Diane —

What a pleasure to meet you. I appreciat your interest in the of the Chelan area — a special place. Best regards,

Sincerely,

Rich Faletto
7/10
Chelan

Four-Eleven!
Pulaskis, Planes & Forest Fires

Manufactured in the United States of America

ISBN 978-1-452-89290-0
Library of Congress Control Number: 2010929629
First Edition

Published by
Richard Faletto
259 Meadow Lane
Sagle, Idaho 83860
faletto@verizon.net

Visit www. fourelevenstore.com

Book cover and interior design and production by BLUE CREEK PRESS
www.bluecreekpress.com • books@bluecreekpress.com

FOUR-ELEVEN!

PULASKIS, PLANES & FOREST FIRES

*A memoir of trail maintenance,
fire fighting and flying on the
Chelan Ranger District,
Wenatchee National Forest*

RICH FALETTO

All photos in this book, unless otherwise noted, were taken by the author.

Cover photo courtesy the Washington Fire Protective Association.

PULASKIS, PLANES & FOREST FIRES

U.S. Forest Service Photo

Bob Lesmeister Photo

Acknowledgements

Several people have helped me research, edit, and bring this book to completion. It has probably taken longer than it should have but the fact that it is finished is a direct result of the efforts of those who have helped me. Here, I wish to honor them for their support and encouragement.

First, my wife Betty deserves top billing for her resolve and gentle urging for me to record these stories. If it weren't for her, I doubt that I would have amounted to much nor would I have ever completed this book. In fact, I probably would not have qualified to receive so much as a library card without her help.

In particular, I wish to thank Bob Lesmeister of Manson, Washington for allowing me to pester him constantly to verify facts, events, locations and other important information. Bob's wife Sue encouraged me to include more sensory observations that I might otherwise have left out. Bob's brother, Terry "Tar" Lesmeister was very helpful in recalling dates and events. Doug Bowie of Wenatchee also deserves thanks for proof reading and insuring historical accuracy. Doug, like Bob and Tar, has a marvelous ability to recall names, dates and locations of fires as well as related events.

Another who has been especially helpful is Bill Moody of Winthrop, Washington. Bill is a well known forest fire Air Attack consultant, former smokejumper and manager of the North Cascades Smokejumper Base. He provided me with valuable suggestions as well as significant information regarding events and fire control operations in the region.

A very special thanks goes to three ladies in Chelan, Washington, who volunteer their time at the Lake Chelan Historical Museum. They are Roberta "Peach" Simonds, Mary Scherer and Linda Martinson. Very early on, Linda urged me to complete this book. She felt that it held substantial local interest, and that it had valuable historical significance. She pointed out that, until now, no one had written about U.S. Forest Service activity in the Chelan area. She suggested that it be done before this information is lost. Linda has not only been a great encouragement, but she has given me countless hours of proof reading and many great suggestions. Peach has been extremely helpful in locating and providing some of the photos contained in this book. Mary Scherer, a former editor, provided early suggestions for editorial improvements.

Tom Leuschen of Fire Vision LLC and Barry George, USFS (Retired) also provided photos and helpful support.

Mallory Lenz, USFS Wildlife Biologist for the Chelan Ranger District fielded questions, provided photo research and good counsel from the very beginning of my efforts. She aided immeasurably in insuring historical accuracy of events described herein. Powys Gadd, USFS Forestry Anthropologist, Okanogan-Wenatchee National Forest, also was especially helpful in locating photos and providing permission to include some of the USFS photos seen in this book.

Dennis King of Dennis King Photography in Coulee Dam, Washington is another who provided invaluable assistance with photos, as did Mike and Randi Hammersberg of Image Maker Photo and Video in Sandpoint, Idaho.

I would be remiss at this point if I failed to acknowledge my publisher, Sandy Compton of Blue Creek Press. Sandy's patience, creativity and professionalism have made this a better book. Thanks, Sandy!

In conclusion, I wish to acknowledge our children Michelle, Peter and Paul who have also urged me to complete this book. Peter, in particular, has persisted in his support and has quietly encouraged me to finish this project. None of them ever fought fire but, both Peter and Paul have several parachute jumps to their credit. Paul is a former enlisted (now an officer) Green Beret who has made many, many jumps around the world over the past 25 years. Like my Mom, I have never been able to figure out why anyone would want to jump out of a perfectly good airplane.

Dedication

This book is dedicated to all of those men and women who lost their lives while fighting forest fires in the mountains of the western United States. Most have heard of the tragic loss of life in the Fire of 1910, the Mann Gulch Fire, the Storm King Fire and, more recently the Thirtymile Fire in the state of Washington. But, many are unaware of the unsung, individual heroes who have made the ultimate sacrifice in the line of duty on less well-known fires. They include two men from Chelan, Washington in the Chelan District of the Wenatchee National Forest. They were Ernani St. Luise, who perished August, 13, 1929 while attempting to save Douglas Ingram, who also became a fire victim, while fighting the Camas Fire in the Grade Creek area above Lake Chelan. Ingram was a Forest Service Range Examiner & Regional Botanist from the Portland office who was sent to the fire as a "Camp Organizer." The second Chelan man was A. K. Platt, a well-known local helicopter pilot who lost his life in the crash of his aircraft, July 8, 1964, in the east fork of Joe Creek while flying back to base from a forest fire on Cooper Mountain.

In memory of:

Source: Kay Platt Thompson

A.K. Platt

Dennis King Photography

Ernani St. Luise

SEARCHERS FIND BODY OF PORTLANDER

Source: US Forest Service

Douglas C. Ingram as he appeared in the costume of the government forest service, prior to leaving August 4 to join the Camas creek fire force in the Chelan national forest.

Douglas Ingram

This marker is located on the Methow side at the top of Douglas Ingram Ridge at N48° 04.159', 120° 09.513'

Source: Tom Leuschen

The markers pictured on this page were placed near the site of AK Platt's crash site in the East Fork of Joe Creek and on Douglas Ingram Ridge where Ingram and Ernani St Luise perished during the Camas Creek Fire. The U.S. Forest Service designed and purchased these markers to honor those wildland fire fighters who lost their lives in the line of duty. The markers were placed by Tom Leushen, Marshall Haskins and Barry George along with relatives of Ernani St. Luise and AK Platt respectively

This marker is located in the East Fork of Joe Creek near Cooper Mountain above Lake Chlan

Source: Tom Leuschen

Source: Bill Moody

This photo was taken of the Thirtymile Fire smoke plume at roughly the same time that the fire swept over fire victims Tom Craven, Karen Fitzpatrick, Devin Weaver and Jessica Johnson. This fire was started by an abandoned campfire that grew to 93,000 acres. The absolutely awesome power of the firestorm created inside of this conflagration is difficult to imagine. It was characterized by high winds, intense heat and highly erratic fire behaviour. And, it produced a catastrophe as tragic as those involving the loss of life at the Fire of 1910, Mann Gulch, Rattlesnake, Storm King (South Canyon Fire) and many others.

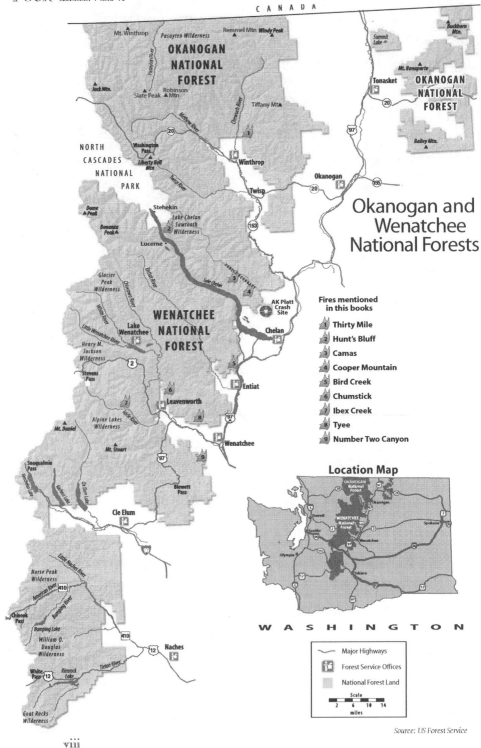

Okanogan and Wenatchee National Forests

Fires mentioned in this books

1. Thirty Mile
2. Hunt's Bluff
3. Camas
4. Cooper Mountain
5. Bird Creek
6. Chumstick
7. Ibex Creek
8. Tyee
9. Number Two Canyon

Location Map

WASHINGTON

Major Highways

Forest Service Offices

National Forest Land

Scale
2   6   10   14
miles

Source: *US Forest Service*

Table of Contents

Source: National Air and Space Museum, Smithsonian Institution (SI 2003-6574).

Japanese "Vengeance" balloon bombs of World War II.

Introduction

'L ead, this is Two. Judy off your starboard, 10 degrees, angels 27."
"Roger Two. Climbing to intercept. Follow me."

The two U.S. Army Air Corps P-38 fighters had just been scrambled from their base at Comox Royal Canadian Air Force Base, Comox, British Columbia and were climbing in hot pursuit of an incendiary balloon launched from Honshu Island in Japan many hours earlier. It was late June of 1945 and America was still at war.

Comox had been quickly alerted to the presence of the intruder by a U.S. Army Air Corps mobile radar unit commanded by then First Lieutenant Hugo W. Schott located at Neah Bay, Washington. Meanwhile, two Forest Service lookouts posted on Pyramid Peak, high above Lake Chelan, Washington, glassed to the west in anticipation of spotting the afternoon sun reflecting off the sides of a mysterious and formidable weapon that was to become legendary in the history of forest fires in the American West.

Obviously, the Japanese intended the balloons to serve as an instrument of psychological warfare as well as a physical threat. Fueled by memories of the firestorms of 1910, the balloons probably created special concern when thought of in the context that there was a shortage of experienced young fire fighters since most of them had joined the armed forces.

The Japanese fire balloons of World War II.

Kept secret by the U.S. from all but those with a need to know, the Japanese endeavor was successful in flying the explosive and highly flammable devices across the Pacific and onto the U.S. mainland. The balloons were constructed of mulberry paper filled with hydrogen and were 33 feet in diameter. The bombs included a cluster of five individual containers which were filled with thermite. Another, larger container held shrapnel. When taken together, what the Japanese had assembled was not only an incendiary weapon, but an anti-personnel bomb as well.

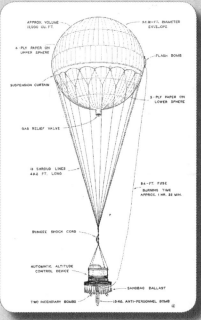

After launch, the balloons travelled over 7000 miles on the jet stream at an altitude of up to 38,000 feet. Some went as far as the mid-west where one detonated over Omaha, Nebraska in 1945 but did no damage. Few fires were ever documented as a result, although one of the airborne bombs did kill six people, including a minister's wife and five children in Oregon. They tampered with the seemingly harmless canisters and the resultant explosion was devastating.

source: www.airmuseum.ca/mag

Another balloon landed in the Hanford Atomic Energy Plant in the state of Washington. It became entangled in power lines and actually threatened to short out a nuclear reactor. Coincidentally, Hanford was the top-secret location where the two atomic bombs were built that destroyed Hiroshima and Nagasaki.

P-38 Fighter similar to the models stationed at Comox, B.C. to intercept and shoot down Japanese incendiary balloons. This particular aircraft was configured as a photo recon plane on a contract mission for the U.S. Geodetic Survey when it stopped at Pangborn Field in Wenatchee in July of 1963.

Except for a few like the two U.S. Forest Service employees who manned the lookout at Pyramid Peak. They had been ordered by the Forest Supervisor for the Chelan National Forest to assemble supplies for two months and pack into the remote lookout in late May. Climbing trees and repairing heavy gauge Forest Service phone line as they went, the two lookouts eventually had to unload and turn loose their pack horses as they encountered snow approximately one and one half miles from their goal. Upon arrival, they had to dig out the structure that would be their home for a couple of months.

The horses, incidentally, made it safely back down from the mountains on their own and later were all picked up by Forest Service personnel.

Mono Faletto, Fire Guard on Jr. Point Lookout circa 1933.

According to my father, Mario A. "Mono" Faletto, who had worked for the Forest Service for 11 years during this period, the two men spent nearly two days of work to clear snow from the lookout and pack in their supplies. Once settled, they opened the manila envelope marked SECRET that they had carried with them, promising the ranger they would not open it until they arrived at the Pyramid Peak Lookout. As one might suspect, their orders were to spot any balloons that got by the P-38s, and

U. S. Army Photo

The Fire Fly Project.

Members of the 555th getting ready to jump.

An interesting result of the concern caused by the Japanese fire balloons was the creation of the Fire Fly Project of 1945. To deal with the Japanese threat, the U.S. Army assembled 300 black paratroopers of the 555th Parachute Infantry Battalion to parachute into the back country to fight fires. During the summer of 1945, men of the "Triple Nickel" jumped on two fires in the Chelan

immediately report them via the Forest Service telephone system to what was then the National Forest Headquarters in Chelan.

In the late 1940s and '50s I heard these and many other stories from Dad as we sat together watching evening lightning storms thrash Stormy Mountain and Slide Ridge high above First

U. S. Forest Service Photo

Francis Lufkin, first jump in 1939, Intercity Airport, Winthrop, Washington.

Creek at Lake Chelan. He loved to watch the powerful and elegant beauty of

National Forest. They were the Bunker Hill and Parks Fires. Francis Lufkin, a pioneer of the smokejumper service, was the jump master for the jump on the Bunker Hill blaze.

Francis and Glenn Smith performed the first fire jump in Region 6, Chelan National Forest, on August 10, 1940. This fire was on Little Bridge Creek in the Twisp Ranger District. The first fire jump

U. S. Army Photo

Operation Fire Fly C-47 which carried members of the all-black "555th" Infantry Battalion on fire jumps in the Pacific Northwest in 1945.

ever was recorded a month earlier (July 10, 1940) on Martin Creek in Region 1, Nez Perce National Forest. Rufus Robinson jumped first followed by Earl Cooley. Dick Johnson, of Johnson Air Service out of Missoula piloted the Travelair which carried Cooley and Robinson onto the pages of history.

the storms, I think, because they brought back memories of simpler and happier times. It was then that I heard the circumstances surrounding the loss of Dad's best friend, Ernani "Nanny" St. Luise, who died in the Camas Fire while attempting to save a Forest Service Range Examiner on the north side of Lake Chelan in August of 1929. This was a "crown" fire which is a forest fire that races through the tops of trees and, in general, does not touch the ground. Most often, it suffocates everything below.

I also heard of Dad's friendship with Francis Lufkin and Francis' attempts to get Dad to join him in the very early years of smokejumping. Apparently, my mother put a stop to that as she viewed the idea of jumping out of a perfectly good airplane that was not on fire, shedding parts or otherwise in trouble as foolhardy.

It was from my Dad that I heard about the Mann Gulch fire and of the extreme danger of "blow ups", a fire that under extremely hot and dry conditions rages into a conflagration that produces high winds and upredictable fire behavior. It is an extremely dangerous fire condition that, sadly, has cost many lives.

Dad also spoke often of his friendship and admiration for Simeon "Sim" Beeson as a smart fire boss. They worked at the Civilian Conservation Corps (CCC) camp at Twenty Five Mile Creek in the late 1930s and they also worked together fighting forest fires in the Chelan area.

The storms and the stories made lasting impressions on me and eventually led to summer employment with the U.S.F.S.

Every once in awhile, one of those storms would produce a lightning strike on Deer Mountain, which was part of the family's 640 acre ranch near Chelan. As a youngster, I often got to see the aftermath of a strike that scarred a large Yellow Pine or Douglas Fir from top to bottom and which invariably produced a small fire. They stayed small because Dad and/or his brothers got to them early and insured that they were out. I remember, on more than one occasion, hearing him field a night time call from the lookout on Chelan Butte with news of a "4-11" (it is repeated as " four-eleven," which is the designated Forest Service radio call to report a fire) on the ranch. Then, he was out the door and on his way to make sure this fire didn't go far. Too young to be invited to go along, I stayed behind and wondered what it was like to fight fire?

This was a time when anyone who advocated "letting it burn" would have been regarded as a candidate for the "looney bin" to put it in the vernacular of the day. Forest Service fire fighting philosophy was grounded in quick response and containment as a result of experience with fires that got out of control, especially those which occurred in 1910.

Young men (and in those days, very few women) who grew up in mountain towns like Chelan, Manson, Twisp, Winthrop, Leavenworth, or Omak knew about fire. They had been taught about the danger of those that went unchecked, and even if they did not work for the U.S.F.S. or the State Bureau of Lands, most knew something about how to fight fire. That was the way it was.

Those who more aggressively pursued work with the agencies charged with fire suppression always seemed to be the ones who brought with them more detailed and practical knowledge of fire behavior and control. These men knew about which way the wind blows up or down a canyon in the morning or evening; they were conscious of the need for escape/safety routes; they were aware of the dangers of crown fires and more. One knew about these things if one came from families like Beeson, Lesmeister, Lufkin, Pino, Croy, Pipkin, Bowie, Moody and many, others.

It was against this backdrop that I began working for the U.S.F.S. in the summer of 1960. I had just finished my freshman year at what was

FOUR-ELEVEN!

then Washington State College (now WSU) at Pullman and I was headed for the Cascades; headed for home at Lake Chelan. Eager to escape classrooms and anxious for the freedom of the mountains, I was exhilarated at the prospect of fighting fire just like others before me.

Chapter One:
Home From College

The most direct route from Pullman to Chelan, Washington leads through the rolling hills of the Palouse wheat country to Colfax, Rosalia, and North to Highway 2; then West through Coulee City and on to Mansfield. From there, on a bright summer day, the Cascades are clearly visible and they beckon for young souls to climb their peaks and ridges and to drink from their cold, clear streams. My pulse always raced at this juncture in the road that took me over the crest of the Columbia River Breaks on the Big Bend and down McNeil Canyon to Chelan Falls. The view of Lake Chelan, and of the family ranch at the base of Deer Mountain from the top of McNeil meant that I was home.

My grandfather, John Faletto immigrated from Italy to Lake Chelan in 1905 looking for his two brothers who were placer mining in the high Cascades above Stehekin. Finding them there must have been no small chore, but he located them in the Lucerne area (King Solomon Mine

1

L.D. Lindsley Photo . Courtesy Chelan Historical Society

***John Faletto (light shirt in back row) flanked by brothers Gus and Sevine
in front of the dining hall at Holden Mine in 1909.***

at Meadow Creek) in 1905. Later, they all worked at the Holden Mine
for discoverer and owner, J. H. Holden. The Holden Mine eventually
produced large quantities of copper while operated by the Howe Sound
Mining Company of British Columbia. It is said the expense of Howe
Sound's mining operation was covered by the gold and silver that was
extracted. Allegedly, the copper was pure profit.

My Father, Mono was born in the little town of Holden in the spring
of 1909. My grandmother wasn't enamored of living with 10 feet of snow

in winter and insisted the family be moved to Chelan shortly after Dad was born . Grandpa purchased a lot and built a home which still stands on Allen Street, from Antonio Pistono in one of Chelan's earliest plats in 1909. He also bought 140 acres of land from Palmer Edwards (previously owned by Luis Muoli) near the Fraternal Cemetery north of town and across from the present day rodeo grounds. While Grandpa continued to work for the Holden Mine, he also placer mined for gold and was involved with a molybdenum claim at Crown Point just below Lyman Lake. He eventually settled down to running the first full service dairy in Chelan. Later, he acquired more land where he raised beef cattle, wheat, oats and alfalfa. He farmed exclusively with Belgian horses and had 15-20 head of draft and saddle horses on the ranch at any given time.

Grandpa was best known for the veal he sold to local butchers, and for the wine he made from grapes

Holden Mine Looks Better

That the Holden copper property on Railroad creek will one day be a great producing mine, is the firm belief of John Faletto, who with his brother last week completed a contract of assessment work on that property.

Mr. Faletto has worked on the Holden for a number of years, having been employed first by the Holden Gold & Copper Mining company and later with the crew employed by the Graves company, and he probably has a better practical knowledge of the mine than any other man not directly interested in it.

The assessment work done under the contract just completed was done in Tunnel No. 3, the big main working tunnel, and was in the nature of a cross-cut driven in the direction of the hanging wall. It was anticipated that the hanging wall would be reached in this cross-cut, but up to the time the contract was completed no evidence of the limits of the ore body had been discovered.

The ore shot out in their work this winter, Mr. Faletto says, is the best in quality he has seen in the mine anywhere heretofore, and although it is still of low grade, it apparently carries large paying values. Tunnel No. 3 has been driven to a longitudinal depth of about 1,700 feet from the portal, and at the point where the cross-cut has just been made in the ore body is about an equal vertical depth below the surface outcropping of the ledge.

To these experienced miners there seems to be no question that suitable transportation only is required to bring this property to the front as a real mine. *Courtesy Lake Chelan Historical Society*

Article in Chelan Leader about John Faletto and the Holden Mine ca 1909.

3

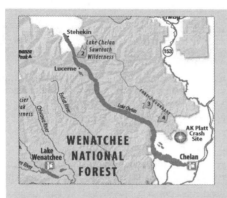

Chelan and surroundings.

The name "Chelan" is derived from pronunciation of the early spelling of the name "Tsillane" attributed to the lake by U.S. Army cartographers. They apparently arrived at this spelling from the name they had heard attributed to the lake by local Indians. To them, Tsillane meant "deep or rushing water". The later was perhaps, a reference to the Chelan River which plunges down a steep gorge, dropping over 350 feet in about 3miles to the Columbia River below. The lake itself is 51 miles long, slightly over 1500 feet deep, two miles in width at its widest spot and about one half mile wide at its narrowest point.

Further up Lake Chelan, and about 30 miles beyond the little community of Stehekin (a Skagit Indian word which means "the way through") an estimated 700-800 men toiled at mining large veins of silver-lead galena ores in the Horseshoe Basin, Park Creek and Bridge Creek areas. For a time, the upper Lake Chelan area was a very popular and active mining area. Long before that it was the way through for the Indians to the Washington coast over Suiattle, Cascade and Rainey passes.

he cultivated from his one acre vineyard. These grapes were planted by the Conti family on a 160 acre parcel that Grandpa had also purchased from Pistono. They originated from cuttings descended from vines in northern Italy nearly 200 years earlier. From these grapes, which were probably Nebiolo, my Grandfather was said to have made the best red, Italian table wine in the region during the 1930s, 40s and 50s.

It was in this farming and ranching environment that I grew up before attending college and working for the Forest Service. I learned to

U.S. Forest Service Photo

Chelan District Ranger Station overlooking Lake Chelan.

ride horses, rope cattle and milk cows at a very early age. I harnessed and hitched draft horses to farm equipment and drove them in the fields. We harvested hay all summer, so it seemed, and we killed 50-60 rattlesnakes every year as we, and our dogs, found them in the shade of oat hay shocks and in other surprising places.

For example, I remember one rattler that crawled into the space between the rear hub and wheel of Grandpa's 1953 Ford pickup. It rode about one mile back to the old ranch house at lunch time. It was "worried" by a barking ranch dog which ran along beside the entire way. The dogs dispatched the unwelcome hitch-hiker when the wheel fell away after I jacked up the truck and removed the lug nuts.

Chelan District history.

There is a long and, judging from the many administrative changes which have taken place there, a very colorful history of forest management in the Chelan region. From 1897 to 1908, the Chelan Ranger District was known as the Chelan District, Washington Forest Reserve. It encompassed a very large area of forest lands including the Chelan, Methow and Okanogan valleys. In 1908, the area was re-designated as the Chelan National Forest (NF). At this time, the National Forest Supervisor's office was located upstairs in the old Miners and Merchants Bank building on Woodin Avenue in Chelan. Later on, in 1910 the Entiat Ranger District was added to the Chelan NF. In 1911 the northern portion of the Chelan NF was split off and became the Okanogan NF. The National Forest Supervisor's office was then moved to Okanogan. In 1921, both the Chelan and Okanogan National Forests were recombined into the Chelan National Forest.

U.S. Forest Service Photo

Helen Giles on First Butte Lookout circa 1953. Very few women worked for the Forest Service in the early years other than as cooks.

Finally, in 1955, the Chelan National Forest boundaries were changed again and it was renamed the Chelan Ranger District of the Wenatchee National Forest. More recently in 2000, the Okanogan and Wenatchee National Forests were combined into the Okanogan-Wenatchee National Forest.

Gifford Pinchot, father of the Forest Service and champion of national parks, visited Lake Chelan in 1897. According to Timothy Egan, who wrote *The Big Burn*, Pinchot called it "a most beautiful trip up this lovely lake." It is noteworthy that the upper end of the Chelan Ranger District was set aside in 1968 as the North Cascades National Recreation Area. The northern boundary of the latter is at High Bridge about 20 miles up the Stehekin Valley. It is at that point that the North Cascades National Park begins.

The excitement of seeing family and friends, coupled with the idea of fighting fire, left me heady with anticipation as I rolled on up the grade to Chelan. As old hands will recall, the business of getting newcomers like me trained and ready to go on a fire line quickly dims any illusions of fun or glory in this risky business. Rather, what I encountered when I reported to the Chelan Ranger District, was a good dose of reality. While we didn't have to make picnic tables or paint garbage cans, we did spend endless hours of boredom sharpening tools, cleaning gear and organizing equipment. Years later, I came to understand and appreciate what a great privilege it was to work for the Forest Service and to have had that opportunity to generate summer income in order to pay for my college education.

The ranger station at Chelan is a beautiful old, lap-sided facility consisting of four buildings (headquarters, two bunkhouses and a warehouse) built in the 1930s. Even today, it evokes memories of a time when forest stewards operated with supreme confidence within the parameters of the day. It projects an air of confidence and credibility that is reassuring and there is

The "Trench."

The Lake Chelan "trench" consists of high mountains on each side of the lake which run 50+ miles into the Cascade Range. When pummeled by winds as it often is, this long narrow valley creates a "venturi effect" which tends to accelerate wind speed. It is nationally known as one of the country's most severe, fire prone areas. Winds here have caused the rapid spread of fire as evidenced by blackened scars which run the length of both the southern and northerly shores of the lake. The terrain is very steep and rugged with few trails and inaccessible heights. It contains volatile fuels, and when paired with the wind, produces extreme fire behavior. Logistically, it is very difficult to fight fire here even with the help of air support, fire boats and transport vessels.

nothing contrived about the building which may, for some, stand in contrast to the modern day penchant for political correctness. Unlike in earlier years, some of today's fires are allowed to burn in areas with excess fuel. Equally foreign to the earlier culture, is a modern day group of Forest Service employees that have organized and call themselves

U.S. Forest Service Photo

This is the sign that Sim Beeson was sanding when he lost his eye.

"Forest Service Employees for Environmental Ethics." Such a movement would have brought puzzled looks and hoots of derision from early western fire fighters. To add to the apparent dichotomy, the heavy wooden Forest Service sign in front of the building is the same one that "Sim" Beeson was smoothing with a power sander without benefit of safety goggles, when he lost his eye to flying debris in the 1940s. Safety goggles were rarely used in those days except by welders and riveters. Today's OSHA would not permit such violations of basic safety practices.

At one time, the Chelan Ranger Station boasted a long wooden dock set on pilings that extended out into the lake. Forest Service boats were tied up there, ready to roar up lake in support of whatever operation was at hand. Exposed to weather — fjord like Lake Chelan is well known for its' devastating winds and waves — the dock was constantly subjected to damage and was eventually removed. Forest Service boat operations were then moved from Chelan uplake to the Twenty-Five Mile Creek Guard Station.

Chapter Two:
Slash Crew and the First Summer

In that first summer of 1960, I was assigned to a "slash crew" that was given the boring task of cleaning up and piling cuttings left by logging operations. The site was on Bear Mountain approximately ten miles from Chelan near the present State Park at First Creek. Our secondary mission was to fight fire should we be called.

The work on a slash crew closely approximates the passion and the fury involved in watching paint dry especially if you are young and eager to fight fire. It is comprised of endless hours of picking up limbs trimmed from logged trees and stacking them on piles to be burned in late fall or winter. Our piles were covered with roofing paper weighted down by tree limbs to keep them dry so they would be completely consumed when burned. The finished job leaves the area clean and park-like, allowing new grass and seedlings to grow and flourish.

A great benefit to our young group that summer involved the knowledge learned about fighting fire from the older, more experienced members of the crew. While our crew boss was David Hale, of Twenty Five Mile Creek, other experienced fire suppression leaders on the crew included Sim Beeson's son Marion, Don Francis and Dean Horton of Manson, Wash. David is best remembered, not only for his impish grin, but for his fire-fighting experience and skill in making the best root beer in the mountain west. Crew members always wanted to be around Dave in hopes of getting an ice cold bottle of his near-famous brew.

On breaks and other times that might fit the moment, younger and less experienced crew members heard of incidents on earlier fires. We listened closely and were given solid advice about what to do in one situation or another. We were warned to always find escape routes in advance of attacking a fire and we were constantly warned to avoid getting ourselves in a situation whereby we might be subject to a crown fire. We were told to always be cognizant of the wind and that breezes always blow up a canyon in the morning and down in the evening.

A "backfire" we were told, had saved Wagner Dodge, the crew foreman at Mann Gulch, and it might possibly save us too if need be. But, we were also taught that backfires could be dangerous and that great care had to be used if it were to be employed.

A backfire is used to burn out areas ahead of the advance of a difficult forest fire, thereby depriving that larger fire of fuel. As one can imagine, this action is liable to create more problems than might be solved, so it should only be used under the right conditions. It worked for Dodge, not because it stopped the advancing flames, but because it created a safety zone (referred to as "the Black") as it deprived the main fire of fuel and diverted it away from him. Thus, he was spared from the killing heat although he suffered greatly from smoke inhalation.

If a fire fighter has to use this method, he or she will want to get into the burned out area as quickly as possible and deploy under a shelter or whatever cover (hat, jacket, tarp etc.) is available. After many tragic fatalities on active forest fires, the Forest Service developed aluminum skinned shelters to protect fire fighters in the late 60's. They have proven effective — if used properly in the prescribed manner and location.

From a practical standpoint, we learned how to use basic fire fighting tools in the course of our daily work. Chainsaws, shovels, Pulaskis (a dual headed fire fighting tool invented by the legendary 1910 fire fighter from Wallace, Idaho) and axes all figured into our daily routine and discussions. The Pulaski is a multi faceted tool that features a mattock on one side of its head and an axe on the other. All of these are first-line fire fighting tools still in use today.

Ironically, Ed Pulaski was never granted a patent for the tool he invented nor was he ever compensated for his expenses or injuries sustained on the Fire of 1910. An unsympathetic Congress also refused his claims for reimbursement of medical expenses that he paid out of pocket, not only for himself, but also for his injured crew members.

Demonstrations about their respective use in cutting fire lines were informative and later proved very effective in actual practice. Surprisingly, there were no personal injuries during this period, but one crew member did manage to drop a rather tall Lodgepole pine across the open rear doors of a brand new Forest Service Suburban. The crew meeting which quickly followed included stern observations regarding safety, common sense, vigilance, and so on. Damage to government property was never well received by our supervisors.

Still, there were no fires for us to fight. 1960 was a hot, dry summer but it produced very few lightning caused fires. Like the old military saying

Bob Lesmeister Photo

Sim Beeson and AK Platt on Lucerne Bluff. As there was not a helicopter landing pad at Lucerne, AK landed in this clearing that was part way up the Domke Lake Trail from Lucerne.

about flying, the business of fighting forest fires "involves hours and hours of boredom interspersed with occasional moments of stark, raving terror." Fortunately, none of the latter ever came our way when I worked for the U.S.F.S. but the fires did come as the summer progressed.

Our first was in late July on a particularly hot day near Wenatchee, Wash. A careless motorist ignited a blaze with a cigarette that eventually burned 1200 acres in Number Two Canyon near Saddle Rock west of the city. The area is steep and covered with Cheat and Bunch grasses, Sagebrush and Yellow Pine. Always extremely dry at that time of year, any fire that is helped by afternoon winds is a problem in the area. Such was

Chelan Valley Mirror — 21 July, 1960, p. 1 — Platt, England injured in helicopter crash.

"Condition improved" is today's report concerning A.K. Platt, Chelan, Leo England of Manson, and H. Stanaway, Entiat, who were injured in a plane crash at the scene of the Wenatchee fire Tuesday.

The three men are in Deaconess hospital where they were taken after the accident. All were in shock, had lacerations, and other possible undetermined injuries.

The crash took place near the Wenatchee Gun club. England, foreman of volunteer fire fighters from this area, had been battling flames since 3 a.m. with nothing to eat or drink. He was in such a state of exhaustion that the helicopter was waved in to take him out.

Platt and Stanaway arrived in the former's helpicopter. England was taken aboard, and the craft began taking off but failed to gain altitude. It came down in a diagonal path, hitting the ground.

Twenty-six cooperators and forest service men from Chelan and Manson were at the fire which covered 1200 acres before it was controlled yesterday morning. The Wenatchee office of the forest service informed the Mirror that mopping up operations were going on and that a close watch is being kept to avoid a new flare-up in the tinder-dry hills.

Local volunteers have returned to their homes, but some of the regular forest crews are still on the job.

Cause of the fire is believed to have been caused by a motorist who had roared up the canyon, turned his car and sped away.

Yesterday Kenneth Blair, Wenatchee district forest service pilot from the Portland office was investigating causes of the helicopter crash, and the fire

Courtesy Lake Chelan Historical Society

Chelan Valley Mirror account of AK's crash in Number Two Canyon.

the case with this one. Crews from Wenatchee, Leavenworth, Cashmere, Peshastin/Dryden and the surrounding areas could not hold fire lines. High winds sent the fire howling over ridges and into brushy draws that exploded with dramatic bursts of flame. Aerial tankers were not available to stop this one and more men had to be assigned to the fire lines. The North Cascades Smokejumper Base dropped four jumpers on this fire along with a trencher. The latter was a gasoline operated machine that dug fire lines in quick order so long as the terrain would allow.

Our crew from the Chelan Ranger District was also mobilized and quickly sent to a heliport established on a ridge about two miles from the

Photo courtesy Kay Platt Thompson

AK in his Waco (similar to a Stearman)) crop dusting an orchard near Manson with Mill Bay on Lake Chelan in the background. It was an aircraft like this (and, it could have been this same one piloted by AK) that took part in testing the concept of aerial fire suppression out of Wenatchee in the late 50s. AK did use this type of aircraft to drop water on an active fire near Entiat in 1959 according to his daughter Kay.

main event. Robert "Butch" Croy and I were the first two from the Chelan crew (others eventually included Jim Thuebet and Doug Bowie) to be ferried across the canyon and dropped off on the fire line. The helicopter was piloted by A.K. Platt, a legend in the aerial fire-fighting business in the region. A.K. was a former U.S. Army instructor pilot who, like a few other pilots in the area, made their living flying Wacos and Stearmans while "crop dusting" local apple orchards.

The following day, A.K. was involved in a spectacular crash when his helicopter went down as he attempted to fly away from a spot on the fire that had accelerated because of increasing winds. A.K. had spotted two men, Leo England of Manson and Haven Stanaway of Entiat, who were trying to outrun that burst. True to form, he picked them up and carried them out of path of the fire. Unfortunately, a combination of too much weight and extreme heat from the fire robbed A.K. of air speed, altitude and good ideas all at the same time. Fortunately, although injured, they all survived, and from his hospital bed A.K. instructed his flagger, Bill Robson of Manson, to call Bell Helicopter and order a replacement for immediate delivery.

A.K. was back in the cockpit and flying again 60 days later. Regrettably, he lost his life in a helicopter crash on a ridge near Cooper Mountain as he returned from taking a fire fighter to retrieve a parked vehicle near a blaze high above Lake Chelan in the summer of 1964.

Ed Armbruster and Dean Kyle were the firefighters who discovered the remains of A.K.'s aircraft in the fire they were sent to suppress the evening that AK was reported missing. The fire burned approximately 30 acres. According to investigators, the cause of the crash could not be immediately determined.

Butch Croy and I were still on the fire line the day of A.K.'s Number Two Canyon crash and all of the next. It was hot dirty work with absolutely no glamour in the work of stopping fire in bunch grass, thick sagebrush and pine thickets. We slept occasionally in depressions in the earth but mainly, we worked continuously to contain the fire. It was here that it became abundantly clear to both Butch and me that our gain was experience and a decent paycheck. There was no real glory in this or any other type of fire fighting.

For the rest of that summer, we continued our work on the slash crew and waited for more opportunity to fight fire and add overtime hours (we were paid straight time) to our paychecks. In the main, the fires of that particular summer were few and small. Most were lightning caused and we got to them quickly. After all, that was the objective of the day.

FOUR-ELEVEN!

Chapter Three:
Preparing for the Backcountry

In the Air Force Reserve Officers Training Corps (AFROTC) program, cadets were required to spend approximately 30 days between their junior and senior year of college in "Summer Camp" at an active Air Force base. This little respite was intended to expose cadets to broader Air Force experiences and more vigorous training in various endeavors. Taking ROTC was mandatory in those years at all Land Grant Colleges in the U.S. As I had decided to become a pilot, I naturally gravitated to the Air Force ROTC program.

Going to summer camp was fun as we were able to fly on a training mission in the USAF's new KC-135 aerial tanker and we got to experience the rigors of the new Survival School near Usk, Wash. The mission had transferred to Fairchild AFB, Wash. from Stead AFB, Nev. Ours was the first class to go through this program. It eventually became the foundation course for survival training and it included exposure and resistance training for the

POW environment. Coincidentally, the navigator on the KC-135 orientation flight was Air Force Reserve Major Ed Armbruster of Manson, Wa. Ed was the Fire Management Officer (FMO) and my immediate supervisor when I worked at the Chelan Ranger Station during that first summer.

Because I was late in arriving for Forest Service summer work in 1961, I was assigned to Trail Crew. This was a fit for all concerned since it allowed time for the snow to melt out of the high country and yet gave me the opportunity for some income to offset college expenses that fall. Most seasonal workers who wanted summer work wouldn't settle for less than a full term, and fewer still were interested in spending the entire time in the back country. It provided little opportunity to fight fire and even less to earn overtime income but, it worked great for me.

When I finally checked in at the ranger station I was assigned various odd jobs involving cleaning, repair and errands. Not much fire activity had occurred and things were relatively quiet for the first few days. Then, just when it was least expected, a brief summer lightning storm swept over the valley. Doug Bowie, temporary lookout on Jr. Point, spotted a lightning caused fire at Safety Harbor on the north side of the lake above Twenty Five Mile Creek. Ray Lesmeister took a "Co-Op"(paid volunteers) crew of fire fighters, including sons Bob and Tar, along with Roger Stafford and John Ward to stop the blaze. Sim Beeson sent me to ride with A. K. Platt in his two seat Bell helicopter to ferry supplies to the site. Before we left, I bought a six pack of cold Cokes for the fire crew knowing full well how much they would enjoy them.

This ride was not my first in a helicopter but I remember being absolutely thrilled to be on board. Summer with the Forest Service had begun! As we flew across Lake Chelan, heading towards Safety Harbor, we encountered a severe down draft and the aircraft plunged straight down, losing several hundred feet of altitude in the process. I lost control of the Cokes in my lap and watched helplessly as three of the bottles sailed out the open door and splashed one after another into the lake below. A. K. just laughed and shrugged his shoulders.

Shortly thereafter, I learned that I would be paired with Bob Lesmeister of Manson for my summer on Trail Crew. I knew Bob by reputation, and he had a good one. He not only was an experienced fire fighter but he was, as they say in some quarters, a "damned good man in the woods." Bob and I hit it off from the start since we came from similar backgrounds, and we were both confident of our respective abilities in the mountains.

This became more evident as we sorted through gear and selected equipment when we outfitted ourselves for the summer's work. For example, I vividly recall Bob passing over machetes in favor of "brush knives" to include in our packs. I wasn't real sure about the reasoning for that move. I didn't know anything about brush knives, but I sure was suspicious of using a jungle tool for mountain work and deferred to Bob's judgement . What I did know something about was horse packing equipment as a result of being around my Dad and our horses on the ranch at Chelan. Bob and I agreed completely on selection of pack saddles, mannys (a tarp used to wrap pack boxes), ropes, halters and the like.

Next came an afternoon of studying maps showing the trails that Sim Beeson had assigned us to brush out and to repair as necessary. They included Domke Lake, Emerald Park, Lightning Ridge, Holden Lake, Railroad Creek and the Agnes Creek Trail systems. We noticed that the last time the trail to Holden Lake trail had been cleaned was 20 years before. Crew members were Sim Beeson and my Dad, Mono Faletto.

Bob Lesmeister Photo

Lady of the Lake at Lucerne in 1961.

Once assembled, we loaded our gear, along with groceries (purchased from Bixby's Grocery on Woodin Avenue in Chelan) for two weeks and our personal belongings on the *Lady of The Lake*, the well-known passenger and freight carrier between Chelan and Stehekin. We then headed uplake for the Forest Service guard station at Lucerne.

Upon arrival, we were to pick up seven burros that the Forest Service had boarded with a local character who had carved out a living as a packer in the area for many years. His name was Oscar Getty. Along with his pal, Gordon Stuart, a true mountain man and a living legend, Oscar was the source of more stories and more hijinks than most hear of in a lifetime. He and Gordon were the resident entertainers at Vic Haight's cafe and bar in Lucerne, especially on Saturday nights. Anyone and anything was fair game for those two and they were well-known for their practical jokes and colorful observations.

Chapter Four:
The Trip Uplake

R iding along on the Lady was, like always, a memorable experience. The day was bright and beautiful; a combination of clean, clear water, azure blue skies, fresh air and the mighty Cascades. Upon leaving Chelan, the lake gradually narrows from a width of approximately two miles near Manson down to around one half mile at the Lake Chelan Yacht Club. Sheer mountain walls reach skyward on both sides of the lake above 25 Mile Creek giving Lake Chelan a fjord-like appearance. From that point on up to Stehekin, the little town at the head of the lake, high peaks and ridges glistened with greenery contrasted by snow above the timberline. It always took my breath away to see this gorgeous panorama again as I knew that, before long, I would be up there. I loved the high country.

As the boat glided on, Bob and I were greeted by first one passenger and then another. It seemed that each had questions about the area and about our role with the Forest Service. It was interesting to talk to these

Upper Lake Chelan viewed from Lucerne.

people as they were genuinely curious about the area and the work of the U.S.F.S. For us, we were amazed at how they had ever heard of Lake Chelan, how far they had come or how they had found their way uplake for that matter. As this summer progressed, we continued to be surprised at the visitors we encountered and at how far they had travelled to reach this area.

Too quickly it seemed, Lucerne came into view and restless passengers began to assemble packs, bags, suitcases and all sorts of belongings to off-load on the dock. Neither Bob nor I were interested in getting off ahead of them but, they were excited and eager to disembark as quickly as possible. We waited until most of them got off and we began to pick up our baggage, which was considerable. We had pack saddles, boxes of groceries, tools and personal gear. I stepped out onto the dock and Bob handed me item after item which I stacked out of the passenger's walk-way as quickly as possible. The Lady needed to sail on up to Stehekin and Bob and I had work to do.

Just as Bob handed me one of the last pieces of gear, he nodded to my right and behind me. I turned just in time to see a young fellow about our age who had picked up one of our chain saws and who appeared as if he was going to throw it into the

Lucerne Guard Station, 1961.

lake. With one quick step, I grabbed the arm that held the saw just as it came forward and pulled downwards. The stranger and the saw dropped straight to the deck. Clearly agitated, he proceeded to lecture me on the fact that "Congress had just created the Glacier Peak Wilderness Area" and that "motorized equipment was not allowed within its boundaries." He was a bit premature (the Wilderness Area was established almost three years later in 1964) in insisting that Congress had created the new wilderness area and he kept insisting we were violating the law.

Finally, after considerable discussion, Bob calmed the guy down and quieted the situation. The intruder left and we moved our gear to the Lucerne Guard Station for the beginning of what became one of the most memorable summers of my young life.

The burro pack string at Lucerne ready to leave for
Domke Lake and Emerald Park in 1961.

Chapter Five
Domke Lake and Emerald Park

After several days of cleaning up around the guard station (manned by Bob as the resident fire guard two years earlier) we set about clearing short, local trails including the Lightning Ridge trail. It was unmarked and used primarily by wild game and by hunters.

Sim Beeson thought it would be a good "shakedown" effort for Bob and me to get accustomed to our equipment. To this day, I will never forget using a crosscut saw to remove many, many downed trees from that trail thanks to the stranger on the dock. It turned out that after our encounter on the dock, he had complained to the ranger in Chelan about the presence of the chain saws we had brought to speed our work.

Neither Gordon Stuart nor Oscar Getty cared for the rules that the Glacier Peak Wilderness area would bring but they both thought it hilarious that Bob and I were obliged to use the crosscut vs. the chain saw. The real joke was that, in addition to the fact the wilderness was only a proposal at the time, the trail on Lightning Ridge was never projected to be within the boundaries of the area after all.

On a bright, crisp Monday morning Bob and I packed the seven burros with our tools, gear and provisions for a five day trip to clean the trail to Domke Lake, Domke Lookout and Emerald Park. The later is a beautiful mountain park high above Domke Lake. Saddling the burros was a piece of cake, but it took at least two hours to pack our supplies and equipment. First, pack boxes were loaded and balanced so that each side of the animal that was to carry the load had equal weight. Manny cloths (a 6'x8' tarpaulin) were then laid on the ground where each pack box was placed upon it, wrapped and tied. These relatively waterproof packs were then securely tied to each side of the animal's Decker saddle with a diamond hitch.

There is no room for error in this process as loose knots or other careless preparations can mean trouble on the trail. Bob and I were very careful about this as slipped packs could mean wrecks that could injure animals or humans as well. In retrospect, we were probably obsessive about the care we took in everything we did. But, as the summer progressed, we found that we just couldn't be too careful. As it turned out, Murphy's Law followed us into the mountains and taught us a lesson or two.

The climb up to Domke Lake was exhilarating as we inhaled the brisk mountain air and reveled in the smells of an early summer day. The burros too shared our sense of purpose and fairly charged up the trail. Well-fed and watered, they were brimming with energy and ready for the day's work. Bob and I were also eager to get on with our tasks and get the season into full swing as well.

Arriving at the fork in the Domke trail, we took the branch which led towards the Domke Mountain Lookout. (This lookout sat atop a 100' tower and the fire guard lived in a small one room cabin on the ground.)

Gordon Stuart's old cabin at Domke Lake.

On we went, marveling at the condition of the trail. From the junction up for nearly one and one half miles it appeared to have been swept with a broom and dusted with pine needles. To be sure, it was the softest walk we ever took that summer!

It finally dawned on us that this was Gordon Stuart's domain and he had taken it upon himself to make sure that the trails around his little corner of the world would be ready for inspection by the most demanding forest stewards. The trail to Emerald Park was an exception, however, probably because it was a steep and rocky path to Gordon's favorite hunting area. Gordon liked to keep it that way to discourage newcomers and to maintain the primitive character of the area for the hunters he guided

27

Milham Pass above Emeral Park. This pass was probably named after George Washington Milham, Forest Supervisor, Washington Forest Reserve, Chelan Division 1901-1915.

up there. Knowing this, we decided to gain time to devote to the harder work ahead, and turned around and headed back to the lake to make camp for our next day's challenge .

As we approached Gordon's cabin, his dog Rupert came bounding up the trail and presented himself to me for a pet, a rub or a scratch as I was in the lead of the pack string. Remembering Gordon's disapproval of anyone showing any favor to his dogs, I told the animal it would be best for him to get away. Besides, I had no idea how the burros would react to the dog or he to them. Further, I had no desire to antagonize Gordon.

But, apparently, Gordon thought I was "courting" the dog and he started yelling at me to leave the animal alone . As it turned out, he mellowed considerably when I re-introduced myself. My Dad had taken me fishing at Gordon's little resort on several occasions where we stayed in one of his cabins on the South side of the lake. He probably didn't really remember me but, he sure remembered Mono Faletto. Gordon got along famously with Dad even though he didn't much care for authority.

At least two to three times each summer, Dad would visit Lucerne and Holden in the course of his duties as a Deputy Sheriff for Chelan County and he made it a point to visit Gordon. He always brought a bottle

Bob Lesmeister making supper on the sheepherder stove in Emerald Park.

of Scotland's finest whiskey for Gordon to enjoy whenever he visited. Gordon knew and liked Bob Lesmeister too, so what started as concern over the dog ended with Gordon being very pleased that Bob and I were there to clean and repair trails.

On we went to the south side of the lake where we scouted the condition of that trail and decided to make camp for our first night out. Mosquitos were thick, but soon Bob had a cooking fire going in the sheepherder stove and the smoke seemed to push them away. We enjoyed what would become one of the most welcome events of our day and that was an evening meal prepared by Bob. Working in the mountains far from civilization tends to accentuate the significance of a social event such as a meal or meeting other people on the trail. For us, meals were something we really forward to sharing and Bob's

Bob Lesmeister Photo

The author on the front porch of Vic Haight's Lucerne Café.

mastery of the sheepherder stove produced some very memorable ones for us.

The next morning we began work on the Emerald Park Trail. It was steep and rocky and no major work had been done on it by a Forest Service trail crew in a number of years. After two days of repairs we walked into Emerald Park in the early evening. It was a breath-taking sight to say the least. The park was alive with color and beauty, including lots of water, snow and green grass. In fact, there was so much snow that it was impossible for us to complete trail work to the top of Milham Pass (named after George Milham, Forest Supervisor, Washington forest Reserve, 1901-1915) above the Park. Hence, we could not place the new trail sign up there that Sim Beeson had sent with us. Our first order of business then was to offload the sign and place it in a log A-frame type of lean-to that Gordon had erected on the edge of the meadow. Once that task was completed, we unpacked the burros, turned them loose to roll and to graze and then we set up camp. Once again, Bob prepared a great evening meal and life was good in the mountains.

Done with the Domke/Emerald Park adventure, we turned back to Lucerne and arrived late on Friday afternoon. As always, the first order of business was to take care of the pack animals. Once finished, Bob and I were able to enjoy the luxury of a shower in the Lucerne Guard Station. The old cook stove cradled copper coils in its heat chamber that warmed water for the bathroom and the kitchen sink. The shower was absolutely wonderful and I will never forget it. First, because the old "technology" was so impressive, and second because of how good it felt on tired muscles.

That night we had a couple of beers, a great meal, and a million laughs with Oscar and Gordon at Vic Haight's Lucerne Cafe.

FOUR-ELEVEN!

Chapter Six:
Lucerne and Railroad Creek

The following week found Bob and me down-lake and working out of the Chelan ranger station as several small fires had been started in the District by lightning strikes. This proved to be a challenge, because in my haste to leave Lucerne, I left my boots at the guard station. This little oversight did not make a favorable impression on the people that I worked for. But, I did manage to borrow a pair from Tony Martinson, a friend and fellow Forest Service employee, and that favor got me by. Normally, I wouldn't share such a rookie mistake but, in this case, it serves a purpose. You see, it provided the push I needed to walk into Polley's shoe store in downtown Chelan and order a custom made pair of White's boots-the "Smokejumper" model.

Now, everyone, and I mean everyone, who I knew that had anything to do with fire fighting at that time wore Whites. Our bosses did, the smokejumpers did and most of us wannabees did too. They provided

Holden Village

Formerly operated by the Howe Sound Mining Company, the town of Holden held over 400 people. The town consisted of administrative offices,

a theater, a bowling alley, a gymnasium, a library, a commissary and a doctor's office. A dining hall was also built that could accomodate over 250 people.

Photo courtesy Lake Chelan Historical Society

Clockwise from above: an aerial view of Holden Village; the main street of Holden Village in 2009; Holden housing for families.

Courtesy Lake Chelan Historical Society

Elbert Hubbard Photo

Holden Village is now owned and operated by the Lutheran Church as a nondenominational retreat.

the toughest and best protection for a man's feet that money could buy. Mercifully, my carelessness gave me the justification needed to buy a pair of boots that were, and still are, the very best for work in the mountains. They were pricey then at $75 per pair but, if you walked onto a fire line wearing Whites, people knew that you were smart enough to take care of your feet and could therefore be counted on to get the job done.

As a matter of interest, I wore those boots for three summers of trail, fire fighting and brush work as well as during the summer in which I flew as an Aerial Observer/Pilot out of the Aerial Fire Base in Wenatchee. I never suffered a sprained ankle or got one blister while wearing Whites. They have been rebuilt once and I still wear them today (50 years later) when I cut firewood or clear brush on my property near Sandpoint, Idaho. They are still like new and "fit like a glove."

When Bob and I returned to Lucerne a week later, we found that a new guard had been assigned to the station and that he had looked after our gear and the burros. Knowing that we would move up to Holden Village in the next couple of days, we began preparations for the trip and used a Forest Service truck to haul supplies up the 12 miles of road to Holden. The Lutheran Church had recently purchased the site along with buildings and equipment from the Howe Sound Mining Company for the sum of $1 . Early-arriving Lutheran staff members graciously allowed Bob and me to cache our supplies there until we could move the burros to the village on our final trip.

That afternoon, a raging thunderstorm swept into the Railroad Creek drainage accompanied by numerous lightning strikes. Once again, Bob and I became fire fighters and back up the road we went to search for "smokes".

Rain began to fall and wisps of fog rose up from the creek below the road. As the evening wore on and darkness descended, we were fooled more

Holden Mine . . . then and now.

The Howe Sound Mining Company operated a large mill at the the Holden mine.

Mill at Holden Mine

Courtesy Lake Chelan Historical Society

The lower picture is what's left of the building.

Sue Lesmeiseter Phto

than once by the plumes of fog that appeared to be smoke from lightning-caused fires. The difference is that smoke from a forest fire has a bluish tint, but the fog is always grey in color. We knew that but were deceived by the receding light. As a result, we took what turned out to be a very long and unnecessary night-time hike down to Railroad Creek only to discover that the smoke we thought we had seen was nothing more than a wisp of fog.

By the time we hiked back up to the road and returned to the guard station it was 11:45 p.m., and we were tired. You can imagine my surprise at finding someone sleeping in my bunk when I walked in. People were sleeping everywhere except in Bob's bunk. He thought it was pretty funny that my bed was occupied, but I failed to see the humor of it all.

The group was led by Floyd Lewman of Manson, and they were co-op firefighters sent to stop any fires the storm may have started. Floyd kindly arranged for his crew member to vacate my bunk and I crawled in and fell asleep immediately. The events of the day and the evening had taken their toll and I was exhausted.

The next morning, Bob and I loaded the burros on the Forest Service truck. They weren't very enthusiastic about the trip and did not conduct themselves like eager, willing travelers. After a "rodeo"(events which included kicking and bucking by the animals) and two round trips up and down the road, we got them safely to Holden. Meanwhile, Floyd and his crew patrolled the area to search out possible fires, and Bob and I set out to establish our base camp for use while cleaning the trail to Holden Lake.

This trail is the same one that we had seen in the records at the Chelan Ranger Station which had last been cleaned by none other than Sim and my Dad, approximately 20 years before us. Since it had not had any attention for such a long period of time, we knew we would have our work cut out for us. As it turned out, we weren't very far off the mark.

View from Holden Lake Trail back towards Holden Village with the Holden Mine tailings pile in the lower center of the photo.

Chapter Seven:
Holden Village and Emerald Park

B ob and I set up camp in a sheltered grove of Douglas fir at the base of an old road that had been started up to Holden Lake but never finished. Our camp was near fresh water, and we tethered the burros to graze nearby. We ate supper and settled in for the night, double checking the burros before we turned in. It had been a long day, and sleep came easily for the two of us.

Next morning, we were up early in anticipation of a particularly active work day. I made coffee and, as was usually the case, I started breakfast and began making our lunches for the day. Bob went to check on the burros and to take them to water. But before long I knew something was wrong as he did not return. Soon, I heard him call for me and I ran down to see what was going on. Bob was leaning over a downed burro that was not moving. This was not a good sign. Evidently, the burro had become entangled in its lead rope, fell over an embankment and broke its neck.

We were heartsick at the loss of the animal, and I felt responsible as I had led the animal to the grazing area the night before. Frankly, I was worried that I would have to pay for it. We were not paid a lot of money, and I didn't relish the thought of the reduction to my paycheck. That is, if I would still have a job after Sim Beeson got through with me. As it turned out, Sim was not happy with the loss but, I did not get fired. We buried the animal and went on with our business.

A month later, Sim recounted a story to me about my Dad who took responsibility for the loss of a horse while working for the Forest Service. Apparently, the horse had died from colic, a condition that prevents a bowl movement . Dad filled out the appropriate forms describing the loss and submitted them to Regional Headquarters in Portland. The forms were returned twice and were marked "Insufficient Justification for Loss" each time. Tired of the bureaucratic merry-go round, Sim took a grease pencil and wrote "Horse Couldn't Defecate" across the front page of the report and sent the whole package back to the Portland office. Nothing further was ever heard of the matter. In checking this story with my Dad, he confirmed the incident, but added that Sim had actually used another, more descriptive word for "defecate" in his reply. I recall that Sim was economical with words, and sometimes colorful. He always was easily understood.

Bob Lesmeiseter Phto

Cutting tag alder along the Holden Lake trail.

We began our work clearing the old road that had

Bob Lesmeiseter Phto

The author with a brush knife on the trail to Holden Lake.

been started years ago and we had a rough time with the "tag" alders as they grew very thickly. In winter, heavy snow compacted them down to chest level and perpendicular to the road. As a result, they developed a memory and continued to grow in that position. Once past the road, we lost the trail for several hundred yards and literally "engineered" our way upwards, choosing a route that made sense in gaining elevation as well avoiding any major dirt or rock-moving efforts. Surprisingly, we connected to the old trail in a draw which contained a spring of cold, fresh water.

Because it was sheltered and cool, we returned to this spot over the next two-three days to have lunch and rest at mid-day. A treat we enjoyed there, which I remember to this day, was a "Fizzy," a cola tablet which we dissolved in the cold spring water. It was the closest thing to a Coke that

41

was to be had in the high country in summer and it was very refreshing!!

Following nearly a week of work, approximately one mile of trail remained to be rebuilt. Sim sent Donald Duby, a young guy from somewhere in the deep south to help us finish. Don was a pleasant fellow and he was

Bob Lesmeiseter Phto

Author with Don Duby in camp at Holden Lake.

also a strong, hard worker who really liked to eat. In fact, he constantly pilfered the camp food supplies looking for snacks. His out-of-cycle consumption depleted food meant for carefully planned and bud-geted meals, and it did not sit well with Bob or me. Don's food binges came to

a halt after the first few days with us as he was abruptly transferred to work elsewhere in the district.

Bob and I reached Holden Lake and set up camp on its shores on a Thursday morning. After turning the burros loose, they grazed contentedly as we walked back down the old trail to finish our work. That afternoon, we kept hearing the "pop" of a small caliber rifle above us. Back at camp after work that evening, we heard the shooting again. High above us, and across the lake from our camp, was a young boy about 14 years old who had come west from Minneapolis. He was here to spend the rest of the summer at the new Lutheran camp at Holden. We called to him to join us for dinner as it seemed better to have him and the gun where we could see them both. The prospect of a hot meal must have sounded very good to him because he climbed down and joined us immediately. He admitted he had been shooting at marmots.

Burros at Holden Lake.

We suggested to him that was probably not a good idea.

Mosquitos were so bad that evening that we pulled large quantities of mountain heather, a vine-like plant with a small flower, and heaped it onto our camp fire. The resultant smoke should have brought a couple of plane-loads of smokejumpers from Winthrop but, thank goodness, the Forest Service lookouts in the area didn't see it because the smoke did rid the little Holden Lake basin of bugs for nearly two days. We were greatly relieved and slept very well that night.

Fly it in, fly it out.

Before we broke camp and left the following day, Bob recalled that the pilot of a float plane from Chelan Airways had mistaken Holden Lake for Hart Lake and had landed there a few years before. Apparently, the pilot was relatively new to the area. Upon landing, he was reluctant to take off again from the little lake and he hiked out to Holden to report his predicament.

He and Hank Harvey, owner of Chelan Airways, walked back in, and so the story goes, tied the tail of the aircraft to a tree at the northwest end of the lake. Hank warmed up the engine, set the flaps, pushed the throttle to the firewall and the other fellow cut the rope. The aircraft barely cleared the tall firs on the southeast end of the lake and Hank flew the plane back to Chelan leaving the pilot to walk out on his own. Standing on the shore, and attempting to judge the margin of error for successfully completing that take off, made Bob and me a little uncomfortable to say the least. While neither one of us was yet a pilot, it just did not look possible.

Our "shooter" spent the night camped near us and left for Holden the next morning to join his group. Bob and I both agreed that it was interesting that he was there alone as well as a bit unusual. We never saw him again.

As we broke camp on Saturday morning, we heard the shouts and laughter of young people coming up towards the lake from the general vicinity of the trail we had just completed. Sure enough, it was one of the first groups of people to come to Holden Village for the summer and they were in the mountains enjoying themselves. We visited briefly with one of the camp counselors who shook his head at the unruly bunch he was "herding." I remember that we moaned about the debris and loose rocks in the trail that came from the newcomers having cut the corners on the switchbacks. But, we were elated at "going out" to Chelan for at least one night for R and R and to replenish supplies.

Bonanza Peak with Mary Green Glacier below the summit.

Chapter Eight:
Hart Lake and Rebel Camp

We were invigorated from two nights in town and rest in real beds
with clean sheets but, now it was time to get back to work. We
had left the burros to graze near Holden and we caught them easily,
packed up and hit the trail. Our initial destination was Hart Lake. This
was the same lake that the new pilot missed on his initial flight into the
Railroad Creek valley.

The burros were feeling good as we pushed up the trail and so were
we. It was a bright sunny day and the grass was green. On the north side
of the trail, multiple waterfalls fell off the side of the mountain and cascaded towards the valley floor. "Shasta" daisies bloomed everywhere. It
was a glorious day in the mountains for us. That is, it was until I experienced the first accident of our summer.

While traversing a rock slide on the trail, a pack saddle slipped on
one of the larger male burros and he stopped. This of course, stopped the

View from Holden Village trail up the Railroad Creek Valley toward Hart Lake.

entire train and I walked back to investigate. As the pack had slipped to the up hill side of the burro, I walked around him and lifted the pack to center it. Down he went with the sharp edge of the pack box pinning my left leg against the rocks on the uphill side of the trail. He couldn't get up and the pain in my leg became worse each time he moved. Since I was pinned, there was nothing I could do to help myself. Frustrated and in pain, I flattened the top of my aluminum hard hat beating on the animal in hopes of making him get up, shift his weight or move enough to provide me with some relief. But, to no avail. He was as helpless as I was and his movements hurt my leg all the more.

Meanwhile, Bob had gone ahead to select a camp site at Hart Lake and could not hear my shouts for help. I was in pain and managed to convince myself that I was injured more than I actually was. By that time Bob

Hart Lake with Crown Point and Crown Point Falls in the distance.

realized that something was wrong and came looking for me. When he finally did arrive about 45 minutes later, I was certain that my leg was broken and that I would get a helicopter ride to the Lake Chelan Community Hospital. I distinctly remember thinking that the area near me on the trail afforded a great helicopter landing spot. Surely, I thought, that will be the way I will leave this beautiful valley.

Reality set in when Bob pulled the cinch on the opposite side of the pack animal and pulled the pack off of my leg. By then, I felt little pain and didn't much care about anything other than getting up on my feet. I stood up on my right leg. My left leg felt numb and was badly swollen to the point that I could barely bend it. Bob concluded that despite the bruises and swelling, it probably was not broken and we should move on to the campsite he had found. It was now evening and the sun was down behind the surrounding peaks.

I used a brush knife as a cane and hobbled along behind the pack string which was now being led by Bob. We soon arrived at camp and set up our tent, built a fire and got supper going. I moved about trying to flex my leg and did my best to contribute to doing chores. By supper time, I felt better and was thankful that the accident was not worse. I was lucky, and my leg, although swollen, recovered quickly.

From this spot on the shores of Hart Lake, we worked our way up the Railroad Creek trail to Rebel Camp. There, we rebuilt a bridge over a two day period. Rebel was situated in a boggy area (caused by flooding beaver dams) at the crossing of a small tributary of Railroad Creek. It had served as a campsite for travelers for many years.

For us, it did not offer much more than a lot of work as the bridge had rotted out and needed replacement. We hadn't counted on this in our plans for the trip and it cost us nearly two full days of hard work demolishing the old bridge; prepping the site, and cutting and fitting big Fir logs as stringers and sills across the creek. We were not equipped for such bridge building activity and moving those heavy logs required a lot of energy as well as ingenuity. A team of draft horses would have helped us immeasurably but, it was up to the two of us and the little burros to move the necessary materials.

We ended up salvaging the old decking planks and reapplied them to the new stringers we had set. The result was a very sturdy bridge that carried horses and pack animals for several more years. We apparently did a good job as Ray Courtney, the well known packer from Stehekin, told us later that he really appreciated the fact that he did not have to lead his pack string through the wet and boggy crossing anymore.

On the last day of work at Rebel, we returned to our camp site to find the burros had gotten into our food stores and had eaten all of our bread (6-8 loaves). As we walked into camp, Lady, the lead burro, stood looking at us. She was an experienced camp thief and added insult to injury with the robbery of our oatmeal, as well as our bread. The loss would later prove to add more challenge and adventure to our summer as we were now short of food. We had little choice

Bob Lesmeiseter Photo

Author with burros packing stringers to rebuild the bridge at Rebel Camp above Hart Lake.

but to clean up the mess the animals had made, prepare supper and plan for the next day's work up Railroad Creek towards Crown Point and Lyman Pass. In retrospect, we were lucky because burros like Lady were fond of eating the labels off of canned foods and this time they left ours alone. Imagine opening a can with no label for breakfast hoping for peaches, and finding sauerkraut?

FOUR-ELEVEN!

Chapter Nine:
Crown Point and Lyman Cabin

Leaving beautiful Hart Lake, we travelled slowly up the trail towards Crown Point. Crown is a well known mining area to those who spend time in the high country, including hikers, mountaineers, miners and Forest Service personnel. It has special meaning for me because my grandfather worked at a molybdenum mine there many years before, and he and his brothers had spent considerable time looking for gold and silver in the area. I had never seen the mine before but, had heard stories about it so I was looking forward to this part of the trip.

It was another gorgeous day in the mountains and we made good time ascending the trail despite having to clear brush along the way. On a large switchback we stopped and spent a good deal of time clearing over-hanging brush from the trail. After awhile I began to smell perfume on the morning breeze. I asked Bob if he smelled it too. He said he did and before long we heard the unmistakable sound of horses. We knew then

*Crown Point Falls with the molybdenum mine tailings pile
(talus slide) to the lower left of the falls.*

that a pack string was coming down the trail towards us. Sure enough, within minutes Ray Courtney appeared carrying four female school teachers from the east coast on a summer vacation trip. They had come from the head of Lake Chelan, up Agnes Creek and over Cloudy Pass . This was one of several incidents we experienced which emphasized how keen one's senses become when away from civilization for several days. It seemed that, not only did our sense of smell became very acute, but so did our hearing.

After having had zero contact with others for several days, smelling perfume and visiting with attractive young ladies was a welcome respite. Ray must have felt a little left out as Bob and I asked the girls all sorts of questions about where they were from and about their trip. Reality

Bonanza Peak.

set in when Ray said they had a schedule to keep, and that they needed to be on their way. Bob remembered we were out of bread and asked Ray to bring us what he could get from the cook in the kitchen at Holden Village. This proved to be a great move even though we had been promised resupply via a parachute drop at the junction of the Agnes and its' West fork near Swamp Creek. That drop was critical to the amount of time we could remain in the high country on this trip.

On our way again, we cut brush and tree limbs that overhung the trail between Hart Lake and Crown Point. The first mile or so above Hart Lake was the worst as it is at a lower elevation with more vegetation. As we approached Crown Point, the undergrowth subsided and we came to the old mine shaft on the north side of the trail.

This tunnel is a popular landmark with hikers and backpackers. It is cut very neatly into solid rock and extends 20-30 feet into the mountainside. There did not appear to be any evidence of minerals or ore nearby that gave us a clue as to what prompted the early miners to expend such effort. Nevertheless, it is an impressive work. Regrettably, it was being used more as a "defecatorium" by hikers than it was as an interesting landmark.

Across the upper Railroad Creek valley we could see the talus slide which dropped from the mouth of the molybdenum mine where my

The Lyman cabin. Note pack saddles and gear hanging under cover on the front porch. This cabin was since demolished to preserve the wilderness feel of the area.

grandfather had once worked. I knew little of his involvement with the claim there, but felt a strong kinship with him and his brothers who also had placer mined in these mountains.

It had been a long day and we were tired. The sun had dropped behind the mountains to the west. When one of our brush knives broke, we decided that we had had a day and it was time for supper. We moved quickly up the trail a mile or so to Lyman Cabin. This old structure was formerly owned by Washington Water Power, a Spokane based utility company, and it had just become the property of the new Chelan County Public Utility District.

Both of these companies used the cabin for winter surveys to measure snowpack in the high Cascades. This provided them with an idea of the volume of water runoff that could be anticipated in the spring. Several photos exist today which show company personnel on snowshoes measuring snow depth near Lyman Lake.

The cabin was also very popular with backpackers and Forest Service personnel as it afforded an extremely comfortable shelter. It was a simple little building made of logs and roofed with split cedar shakes. The floor was made of rough sawn planks. Outside, it featured a rustic, covered porch and a couple of windows. Inside was a simple cook stove, a table and chairs and two large bunk beds.

Soon after we arrived, I unpacked the burros while Bob made supper. By the time that I had the packsaddles hung under the porch (this kept them dry and above all, away from chewing rodents like porcupines and wood rats) I could smell the food Bob was cooking. A typical evening meal for us would be canned meat, canned vegetables, bread and canned fruit for desert. Whatever was on the menu was always a feast after a hard days work. Typically, we probably consumed 3500-4500 calories per day to maintain the level of activity necessary for the type of work we did in the mountains.

After we ate, Bob set about burning a hole through the brush knife handle that we salvaged from the break earlier in the afternoon. The head of the knife attached to the handle shaft via a sleeve held in place by a single bolt. It was at the bolt hole that the wooden handle had snapped. Bob had found a large steel nail that was roughly the size of the bolt and he heated it in the cabin stove until it was white hot. After repeatedly heating, and then burning the hot nail into the handle, he succeeded in creating a hole. This allowed reattachment of the head which was then secured by the original bolt. We were back in business, but with a brush knife that was slightly shorter than the original. This was the first of several repair jobs that Bob and I accomplished far from civilization which

Lymna Lake with the remnants of Lyman Glacier in the background.
This glacier once filled the entire basin above the lake and had gradually
receded to the size shown in this photo taken in 1961.

resulted from what we called " Good old Yankee ingenuity!" Common sense, luck and availability of needed materials are essential to making repairs in the back country.

The next morning, refreshed from a good night's sleep and a hearty breakfast, we hiked back down the trail to finish cleaning the section above Crown Point. Done by mid afternoon, we returned to the cabin in anticipation of a bath in the waterfalls nearby. Two years earlier Tom Moody, Jim Paulson and Phil Clark, the Forest Service crew that preceded us in cleaning this particular trail, had also stayed at Lyman Cabin. They told us of the waterfall on the nearby creek and Phil mentioned a waterslide where the stream cascaded over slippery rocks. So, we had the promise of not only of a little fun, but a bath to boot. We never did find the slide, but we did enjoy the bath.

When the three that preceded us left the cabin to cross Cloudy Pass, they encountered a Sierra Club writer and a photographer from National Geographic Magazine. They were exploring the North Cascades for the purpose of preparing a feature article. When it appeared several months later in March of 1961, the magazine carried a photo which showed the crew leading a pack string of burros through the meadow just below the east side of Cloudy Pass. It is a beautiful place and the photo of the pack string was accentuated by green grass and flowers against a backdrop of very rugged mountains. The fact that this photo of three guys that we knew had appeared in a famous national magazine made a lasting impression on us.

Later that evening, a boisterous and very loud thunderstorm settled on the area. It poured rain in a way that I had only seen west of the mountains in the Seattle area. We were snug in that cabin though, despite the bright flashes of lightning and the roll of thunder. That is, until someone began pounding on the door about 1AM.

Bob got up and looked outside. There stood a man and his two daughters, all with backpacks and slickers. They were wet and cold as they had hiked all day from the west side of the mountains up and over Suiattle Pass, then over Cloudy Pass to the Lyman Cabin. Obviously, they needed shelter and of course we invited them in. They appreciated the fact that we shared the cabin and thanked us repeatedly. Bob and I gave up our bunks for the girls and we slept on the floor for the remainder of the night.

Bob and I packed up and left very early that morning while our guests remained asleep. It seemed fitting that it was foggy and cloudy when we crossed Cloudy Pass a couple of hours later.

Bob Lesmeister leading a pack string across Cloudy Pass. Note the abundance of wildflowers in the meadow. A similar photo of a Forest Service pack string in this same spot appeared in the March, 1961 National Geographic.

Chapter Ten:
Cloudy Pass and the Agnes and Swamp Creek Trails

The trail was easy and clear of brush on the Agnes Creek side of the pass. The burros felt good and moved along at a good clip. When we reached the valley floor grass was abundant and they snatched bites as we moved along. Our destination was the camp site at the juncture of Swamp Creek and the main Agnes drainage. That was the place that we were supposed to find a message which was to confirm the parachute drop of food which would have allowed us to continue up the West Fork of Agnes Creek to spend a week cleaning that trail.

We moved at a brisk pace through the high meadows at timberline and on down into the first stands of scrub timber. As we began to encounter taller trees further down we also found more brush and debris to remove from the trail. Suddenly, there was a tremendous crash behind us and the burros jumped at the sound. We were as startled as they were at the noise in that very quiet valley. We looked back up the trail and saw a huge dead fir snag had fallen across the trail in a spot we had just passed. Had we or the burros been it's path, there surely would have been a fatality and/or injuries. This incident had a very sobering effect on both of us, and after removing the debris, we moved on engaged in our own thoughts.

Arriving at Swamp Creek, we set up an overnight camp and went fishing as we were short on provisions. There was no message there regarding the food drop so we knew that all we had time to do was to clean the shorter Swamp Creek Trail. The prospect of fresh trout for supper was appealing and we were not disappointed.

As the burros had eaten all of our bread the prospect of several days of hard work up Swamp Creek was not an especially welcome thought. Nonetheless, we packed up that trail the next morning, built our camp and set about the work at hand.

We knew a little of what was ahead of us. Bob's dad Ray had looked for gold in the area the year before and had mentioned that heavy snow slides had destroyed the trail in two places. Whoever was to clean it was in for some "tough going" he said. And, he was right. It was a difficult trail to clean.

Ray also mentioned that there was a cabin at the high end of the trail. He also mentioned that he had spent a night or two recuperating inside it after a rock had fallen on his hands. We thought it might afford us shelter as well, but it took us two full days to reach it, cutting downed timber and moving rocks left by the snow slides over the trail. Our chain saws were woefully inadequate for the job as they both had only 16" bars. They were just too small for the task. Eventually, we did open the trail, but not without considerable effort, and on "short rations" as well.

On the evening of the second day, I hiked back down from Swamp Creek to the junction with the South Fork of the Agnes. I went to see if Ray Courtney had left us any supplies. As mentioned earlier, Bob had asked him to bring us bread from Holden Village. Sure enough, Ray had left us a loaf of bread as well

The "hungry camp" at Swamp Creek. The valley was so steep that there wasn't a flat spot to set up the tent other than right on the trail itself.

as our mail. He also left us a note from Sim which indicated there would be no parachute drop and confirmed we should clean the Swamp Creek Trail.

As might be expected the bread lasted for a very short time and Bob and I ended up living on pancakes for three days. We had pancakes for breakfast, pancakes with peanut butter and jelly for lunch and pancakes for supper. By the time we opened that trail all the way to the old miner's cabin, we were very, very hungry, and we had a long way left to go to get to a source of supplies in Stehekin.

FOUR-ELEVEN!

Next morning, which was a Saturday, we had coffee and our last can of fruit for breakfast. We broke camp and started down for the High Bridge Guard Station. It was approximately a ten mile trip. We arrived about four in the afternoon and took care of watering and feeding the animals from a stock of hay in the barn and went into the guard station. Lo and behold, there was the food that was supposed to be air dropped to us along with another note from Sim advising us to move on up to Park Creek Pass to clean that trail. I read my mail that had been left with our groceries and Bob attempted to call the guard at Stehekin on the old crank operated, battery phone. After our extended time in the mountains, we really wanted to spend Saturday night and Sunday in town.

As I was reading a letter from my girlfriend, a vehicle pulled up and a man began unloading a backpack. He didn't notice that we were there nor did he seem to expect anyone to be at the station. Since no one in the Forest Service had heard or seen us for some time (Ray Courtney had confirmed to Sim that we were up in the Swamp Creek area) Bob's dad decided to come looking for us. The Lesmeisters owned a cabin at Stehekin along with the old pickup he drove to find us that day. In his pack was fried chicken that Bob's mother had sent along. It was great to see a friendly face, but I can assure you that we were even more interested in that fried chicken.

Once down to Stehekin, Bob and I showered, put on clean clothes and had a great meal in Beryl Courtney's café. It was topped with her famous Washington Nut Pie. Sim Beeson flew in on Chelan Airways just about the time we finished dinner. His first comment was "Where in the Sam Hill have you two been"? As one might imagine, the response was an equally blunt question as to why he had tried to starve us to death by neglecting to air drop our groceries.

Always the boss, Sim made it clear that he had had to make a decision about allocation of air resources and, regrettably, it had not favored us. There was a lesson there, and he made a point. Sim was a highly respected leader and while he might have been a little rough around the edges, we loved the man. The next afternoon, he insisted we take his boat and spend the afternoon waterskiing. That was Sim!

Jim Thuebet in before and after pictures of clearing the Flat Creek Trail.

Chapter Eleven:
Flat Creek Trail and Cedars

O ver the weekend, he had told us that our next assignment was to clean the trail into Flat Creek. He also told us that we would have a new companion for this job and that he would be my old duck hunting partner and former smokejumper, Jim Thuebet. Jim's parents were wonderful people who owned the Sand and Surf Restaurant in Chelan and they were always very good to us when we came in looking for Jim.

Early Monday morning, we loaded our supplies and gear in the Forest Service pickup and headed up to High Bridge Guard Station where we picked up the burros and pack equipment. From there, it was about 7 and 1/2 miles to the mouth of Flat Creek where it empties into the Stehekin River. About two miles downstream from the mouth of Flat Creek is the point where Bridge Creek empties into the Stehekin. Bridge Creek is a well known drainage in the area and is an important route on the Pacific Crest Trail just like Agnes Creek.

Bob Lesmeiseter Photo

The author cooking breakfast at Flat Creek Camp.
Jim Theubet's cocker spaniel supervises preparations.

We finally matched up burros, pack gear and our supplies and waded across the Stehekin River around noon. Jim brought along his little black Cocker Spaniel and he had quite a time getting across the Stehekin. His legs were so short that he couldn't wade very far so he had to swim. The current made his crossing a real chore for him.

Jim Thuebet at Flat Creek.

We stopped on the far side to wring out our socks and pant legs and then hiked about 5 miles up the Flat Creek Trail. This area is heavily forested with big Douglas fir and cedars.

66

Flat Creek cedars.

Surrounding our Flat Creek Camp was a grove of huge cedar trees, a few of which had had large slabs of bark peeled off (approximately three feet by six feet in size) many years earlier. The thickness of the callus growth around the border of the cuts indicated that the bark had been removed long ago. We speculated that this had been done by Indians in order to harvest the bark for making baskets. Or, perhaps it was done by a prospector or trapper who used it to build a quick shelter? This was a special place and we felt a profound sense of respect for it.

Bob Lesmeiseter Photo

The huge cedars at Flat Creek.

The trail was mercifully clean all the way to the first major crossing of the creek. That is where we set up our camp for the next two weeks.

The large cedars grew close together and their root systems held the bank together at this spot. Flat Creek bent around them here and flowed

67

on towards the StehekinRiver (leaving us a large pool from which to dip our cooking and drinking water.) It was a perfect spot to locate a camp. We quickly set our wall tent and arranged the pack boxes in a secure manner. It was designed to keep the burros from perpetrating a day time raid on our food when we were away working on the trail. This would be our home for the next two weeks and we did all we could to make it comfortable.

We then left to determine what would be needed to clear the trail all the way past the old fire camp that Sim had described. Years earlier, he had led a fire crew into the area to fight a blaze just below the Flat Creek Basin. He told us that we would recognize the spot by the depressions dug in the ground that served as bed locations for the crew. After a good hike, the trail disappeared in a tangle of brush and small firs. A little further on, sure enough, there were the tell tale "beds" left by Sim's fire crew. At this point, it became abundantly clear that it would take two full weeks to clean up this trail and make it passable once again.

Back in camp it was time for supper, and once again Bob performed his own brand of mountain magic with a hot meal that was absolutely superb! We had had a long day and sleep came easily for all of us...until the visitor entered our tent sometime during the night. I awoke to the sound of "g-naw, g-naw"; or to put it more succinctly, the sound of an animal gnawing on something. I shined my flashlight in the direction of the noise and there sat a big, fat porcupine chewing on what was left of Jim Thuebet's 35mm camera case.

As the others stirred, I yelled "look out, there's a porky in the tent". With that announcement, all hell broke loose. There was a great deal of commotion as all of us tried to avoid the critter. In the meantime, the porcupine, was equally determined to get away from us. Needless to say, we were concerned at the possibility of getting too close to sharp quills and that left little hope for much sleep that night. To this day, I consider it a minor miracle that Jim's dog did not try to attack the big rodent.

In the morning, we saw that the damage was worse than expected. This porcupine had a taste for sweat soaked leather (it is salty) that defied imagination. Not only had he chewed on Jim's camera case, but he severely damaged pack saddles as well. This would not do.

The 1961 Trail Crew (l to r): Bob Lesmeister, Jim Thuebet and Rich Faletto

After breakfast we hoisted our leather gear up into the trees and we secured all other items that might fall victim to our nocturnal friend. Only then did we resume our efforts at rebuilding and reclaiming the Flat Creek Trail.

That night, we retired early and were asleep in no time. That is until about 2-3 in the morning when Bob yelled, "Look out, that darned porcupine is over by you, Jim." Sure enough, it had returned and was just about finished eating the remains of Jim's camera case. All that was left of it were the two metal snaps that secured the hood that folded over the top of the camera. Out the tent it went with Bob and me in hot pursuit. This time Bob saw it run (they are faster than one might expect) under a downed fir and into a rock slide behind the big cedars. Again, we slept fitfully. We were beginning to getting cranky because of lost sleep caused by the "thief in the night."

All the next day, tempers were short. Dirt, rocks and brush flew out of our way with a vengeance. Late in the afternoon I confided to the others that I had a .22 cal. revolver in my pack and that it was time for us to stop the varmint from doing any further damage to government property, or to us. Before we went to sleep, I positioned the gun so it could be reached by any of us should the visitor return. Sure enough, at about 3 AM, the porcupine came back into the tent. Bob was first to awaken and when he reached for the revolver, the porky ran out of the tent. Bob was quick to follow with me right behind. He was able to fire two rounds into our tormentor before it got into the rock slide. We slept much better that night and were never bothered again by unwelcome critters in our tent that summer.

Chapter Twelve:
Flat Creek History

The remaining time in Flat Creek was uneventful as we worked at our task. The area is incredibly beautiful and, as mentioned earlier, holds stands of the largest cedar trees I have ever seen in the inland northwest. They rival those in the groves located near Priest Lake and Bonners Ferry, Idaho. The three of us all took several photos of these giants, and we still remain in awe of their monstrous size.

After our first week, we were able to return to Stehekin and enjoy the weekend. It was indescribably wonderful to enjoy a hot shower, wash clothes and have a home cooked meal at Courtney's cafe. On Saturday night we were treated to an outdoor showing in the little Stehekin community park featuring an old "Lassie" movie (The Courage of Lassie) which had been filmed nearby. Then, "Skinny" Wilson invited us over for dinner, some of his famous home brew and a round or two of poker.

On Sunday evening we caught a ride back up the road to the Stehekin River/Flat Creek junction. There, we shared a watermelon with two girls

Flat Creek mystery.

The area is of historical significance, and in it we saw clear evidence of prospector's work, trapper's lines and possible Indian activity. A few years after we cleaned that trail, the pilot of a helicopter on a geological survey landed in the Flat Creek Basin. After shutting down the engine, he walked around the area, presumably searching for ore samples. He eventually stumbled upon an old prospector's camp. There he found a human skeleton, a frying pan and what was left of an old Winchester rifle leaning against a tree. To my knowledge, the remains were never identified.

from Chelan as we sat around a campfire. They returned to Stehekin that evening and we rolled out our sleeping bags and slept under the stars that night. Crossing the river at daylight, we were back at work on the trail within a couple of hours.

Two days later, after a particularly tough day of removing trees and brush from the trail, we hiked back to camp in anticipation of one of Bob's great suppers. The burros had crossed back over Flat Creek (we had herded them across to the north side of the creek to keep them from raiding our food boxes again) and were nosing around in camp. We immediately started yelling at them and throwing rocks across the creek to run them out of camp.

All of a sudden, there was a good deal of cussing and a head popped up around a tree near our food cache. It was Sim! He had hiked in to check on our progress and was looking for something to eat. The burros sensed a free meal and were all too happy to greet our visitor in hopes of a handout.

Surprisingly enough, we never had an animal get into our food boxes (aside from the burros) that entire summer. In retrospect, the boxes would not have denied access to a bear, a wolverine or a cat, but we did not see any of those animals that summer.

A few years before, I asked my grandfather if there were bears in the high country at Lake Chelan in the early 1900s. He answered in the affirmative. "There were lots of them, both blacks and silver tips" he said. When I asked what happened to them, he shrugged, and he said that "We shot them because bears and people don't mix." Old timers often referred to grizzly bears as "silver tips."

Bob Lesmeister Photo

Bob Lesmeister operating the "Punjar" on Cascade Pass.

Chapter Thirteen
Park Creek Trail and Park Creek Pass

After finishing the Flat Creek trail we returned to Stehekin for another weekend off before our next assignment. Bob and I were surprised when Sim told us over coffee at Courtney's that he was splitting us up and sending Bob up to Cascade Pass to work with a crew there. Bob was an experienced powder man and "Punjar" (a brand of jackhammer) operator and Sim needed him on the effort to build new trail through rocky terrain. He then said that Jim Thuebet and I were to pack up and clean the trail up to the top of Park Creek Pass.

Park Creek is one of the most beautiful places on earth and Jim and I were thrilled to get the assignment. We had no way of knowing that it would turn out to be a difficult challenge for both of us.

Ron Johnson was the Fire Guard at Stehekin that summer and he drove us, along with our food and equipment, to the Park Creek trailhead. It is located about a quarter mile above the mouth of Flat Creek on the

View from near the top of Park Creek Pass looking back down the narrow Park Creek drainage toward the Stehekin River. Buckner Mountain, to the right, and Booker Mountain, straight ahead.

Stehekin road. Fortunately, the burros had remained in the same vicinity where we had left them to graze two days before. There they were, seemingly pleased to have our attention and get back on the trail again.

Again, Jim brought along his cocker spaniel. The little black dog didn't cause any trouble in Flat Creek, but this time I was concerned. A prior experience had taught me that mixing dogs and pack strings in the high country could spelled trouble. As it turned out, one of the burros liked the idea even less than I did.

It was a bright, beautiful morning and we packed up quickly. Soon, we were on our way up the many switchbacks from the valley floor. It seemed that we gained the elevation which got us above the steeper segments very quickly. The trail leveled off, traversing more gradually than in the earlier part of the climb. The first mile was not a "walk in the park" as they say, and all of us were feeling the effects of exertion. In the dog's case, he wasn't paying attention and followed the rear animal too closely. The burro delivered a solid kick that connected with the little black dog's head. He yelped and rolled over. Blood ran from his mouth. There were a few anxious moments for me as I am an animal lover and didn't relish the idea of the dog being hurt. Jim, on the other hand, waved it off with typical nonchalance. He said the dog would be just fine.

And, he was, but it took a rest and water from the canteen to get the animal to continue on up the trail. It must have been a good lesson for him because that dog gave the burros a wide berth from then on.

Two Forest Service "cowboys" – Jim Thuebet and
Rich Faletto – in Park Creek Basin.

Finally, after a steep uphill climb of about two more miles, we arrived at the camp site which sits at the only crossing of Park Creek itself. It is in a narrow defile and provides a welcome "traveler's rest." It would serve as that as well as an "infirmary" on the return trip.

After a nice meal, we turned in and got a good night's sleep. Up, packed and on our way again the next morning, we continued up the trail towards our next camp site in the Park Creek Basin. This is a gorgeous location at the foot of Park Creek Pass. It is bounded on the West by Buckner and Booker Mountains and by Storm King and Goode Mountains to the East. When we arrived in the early evening, the sun had sunk behind the peaks. Grass was green and thick there, and the burros were content as they fed around our campsite.

The next morning we set about to clean the last portion of the trail. Fortunately, we were high in the alpine country near timberline and there was very little brush to contend with. After returning to camp for lunch, we hiked up the trail in the afternoon to the top of the pass. The path itself winds its' way up through rock slides and over the pass to Thunder Creek on the North side. It was in good shape, as might be expected in

Bad judgement and an early winter.

Sim told us the story that years earlier, a packer had come up Thunder Creek in late September with a load of supplies destined for the mines at Horseshoe Basin. He got caught in a blinding, early season snow storm and lost his animals in deep snow. All perished except the packer who made it out alive. There, above us in the saddle, and just under the top of the pass, we saw the bleached white bones of many horses. It was a chilling sight which carried a warning and left a lasting impression on me about not taking unnecessary risks.

an alpine area, although we did have to move some rocks in order to improve passage. It was much easier than dealing with the logs, trees and Tag alders of earlier trails that summer.

Just as we turned to head back to camp, a tremendous clap of thunder echoed through the mountains, almost as if to add a punctuation mark to what we had just seen. Coming back down the pass, we noticed that a new camp had been set up above ours and we stopped by to say hello. It turned out that the camper was a political science professor from the University of Wisconsin there with his family to enjoy the high Cascades. After a brief visit, we headed down to our tent as it began to rain.

We crawled into our tent, which was not large but adequate for two people. Since it began raining so hard, we did not build a fire to cook supper but instead ate some candy bars to tide us over for the night. We got into our sleeping bags early and read for a couple of hours. I had brought along a small am/fm battery powered radio and we were able to listen to radio station KJR in Seattle. It was interesting to think that my girlfriend, Betty, was probably listening to the same tunes — *Smoke Gets In Your Eyes, Louie, Louie* and others — that we were hearing that night.

Tired of the static produced by constant lightning, I finally turned the radio off. A break in the constant downpour of rain produced a silence that was very unusual that evening. All of a sudden there was a thunderous crash of thunder and followed by a flash of lightning that made us jump. The sound was all the more dramatic as the valley walls are so narrow, and they seemed to confine the noise to the area around us. It seemed that the storm went on for hours.

When I awoke in the morning, it was still raining. The evening before I had positioned our little sheepherder stove under the tent flap just outside our door. I also placed a small amount of dry wood under cover nearby. There was just enough to boil water for oatmeal and I soon had a fire going and water boiling. After a quick breakfast we broke camp, packed the burros and headed down the trail.

As we had completed most of the trail maintenance on our way in, there was little left to do on the way out other than to cut a little brush here and there. I favored using the brush knife that I had used all of that summer. I was in the lead, using it as we walked down the trail. Jim was in the rear of the pack string and he carried a machette that he could swing with considerable authority. He was in great shape and one tough trail crew man.

After awhile, we switched places, as was customary. I left the brush knife with the lead burro and walked back to Jim's position where he had left his machette. I didn't like it, and I was very careful when using it. But, it was dull, and I couldn't cut brush with it.

I asked Jim to stop so I could sharpen the blade . After I finished, it would cut through anything I targeted like a hot knife through butter. I couldn't figure out how Jim cut with it other than with sheer, brute strength.

After an hour or so, we switched places again, and I was glad to have the brush knife back. And, away we went again. The sun came out and we made good time on the downhill run. So good in fact, we thought we would make it all the way out to the Stehekin road that afternoon. Then it happened.

We were just passing a small clump of willows which were growing out of a stump that had been cut a few years before. Below the clump was a granite boulder imbedded in the bank of the trail. Jim noticed the willows as he passed he cut them off with one mighty swing.

Remember that I had just sharpened the machete and it would not take the amount of energy that Jim had been expending earlier to cut through this growth. His swing carried completely through the willows, glanced off the stone and hit his knee diagonally from above the top of his right kneecap to just below it. His yelp of pain got my attention and I wasted no time getting back to him.

He was on the ground and grimacing while holding his leg. Fortunately, bleeding was slight. Nevertheless, I immediately had him clench his hands together and put them between his thighs while I put weight on them in an attempt to slow what bleeding there was. This I had learned in Boy Scouts and I was grateful that I paid attention on my way to earning a First Aid Merit Badge a few years earlier. I fastened my belt around his legs above his knees to maintain the pressure on his clenched hands and then slit his pant leg from boot top to the wound so I could treat it more effectively. Jeans were tight in those days and there was no way to pull Jim's pant leg high enough to reach the wound. I declined to ask him to pull them down.

I did my best to avoid letting Jim see my reaction to the wound, but to be truthful, I was worried. The cut was so deep I could see bone and what appeared to be tendons or muscle. Some bleeding continued despite the makeshift tourniquet that I had fashioned. Jim was a real trooper though, and he made it easier for me to work.

As the flesh had separated widely at the wound, I first cut strips of tape and applying them to force the wound to close. On top of these tape sutures I applied a sterile compression bandage and taped it down. I then wrapped the whole thing with gauze tape from the first aid kit. Then, I finished off the dressing with a splint made from a board from one of the pack boxes to help keep Jim's leg immobile. The bleeding had stopped, but I did not want to aggravate it on the trip down the mountain.

There was no way that Jim should attempt to walk so I unloaded the gear from our largest and gentlest burro so he could ride it out. I redistributed the load onto the other animals and we started down the trail again. Apprehensive at what might lie ahead, I alternated leading the pack string and checking on Jim. To my relief, things went well and we made it to the camp at the creek, crossing around 5PM that evening. There was a log across the creek and Jim shinnied across, staying dry and avoiding more problems with his injury.

I made Jim as comfortable as I could, and soon had a shelter up and a warm fire going. As I began to heat a canned ham for dinner, three men walked into camp. They were all professors from the University of Oregon and, as I recall, they all taught in the Dept. of Psychology. It was great to have some company, especially considering Jim's accident.

One of the newcomers was a Phd. I remember wishing he was an MD as I was concerned about Jim's leg and uncertain of the effectiveness of the first aid I had rendered. We visited for awhile and they then moved up the trail to a site just above us and set up their own camp. Just before we ate, one of them came back with a pint of bourbon whiskey and offered Jim a drink. By the time supper was ready, Jim was quite relaxed.

We slept well that night and got an early start in the morning. Jim's leg was stiff but he did not seem to be in as much pain as the evening before. Arriving at the Stehekin road about 2PM , I helped Jim off his burro and unpacked the others which I turned loose to graze. Just then to my surprise, and much to my relief, I heard a vehicle coming. Sure enough, it was the Stehekin Fire Guard, Ron Johnson. He told us that he had had a premonition the night before that something was wrong with us. He was still so concerned in the morning that he came up looking for us — one full day earlier than planned.

We loaded all of the pack gear in the back of the pick up and perched Jim on top so he could stretch out his leg and relax. Ron mentioned that there was a doctor vacationing in Stehekin and that is where he took Jim. The doctor (Dr. Fred Bowles) was a pediatrician but he examined the wound. He said that it had begun to heal "nicely". He then dressed it with clean, fresh bandages and sent Jim on his way. Sim arranged for a flight to Chelan for Jim with Ernie Gibson of Chelan Airways so he could be examined at the local hospital. He was doing so well that he quickly went back to light duty at the Chelan Ranger Station.

Ron Johnson, Stehekin Fire Guard on the Hunts Bluff Fire downlake from Stehekin.

Meanwhile, lightning strikes from the storm that passed over Jim and me up in the Park Creek Basin had started fires in the Stehekin area and also down at Chelan. Bob was called back from Cascade Pass and a fire crew was sent up from Chelan to help us with the Hunt's Bluff Fire just downlake from Stehekin.

This fire was located on steep, rocky hillsides that were full of brush and dry grass. There were a few Yellow Pines- Ponderosas- that burned within the perimeter of the fire, but fortunately, we did not have to deal with the type of conflagration associated with a fire in heavy timber. And, thank goodness, we were not plagued by the aggressive winds that are characteristic of the area during hotter, summer months.

This fire was difficult to suppress because of the terrain but, a fire crew including Roger Stanford and John Ward, and led by Darrel Wilsey, got to it early and had it under control by the time we got there. Ken Saunderson picked us up in the Forest Service boat which we loaded with coils of hose and two gasoline operated pumps. After setting up that equipment, we

A lightning stike caused this fire on Cooper Mountain. Evidence of the strike is visible as a thin line down the lighter-colored tree in the center of the photo.

pumped water up the steep hillside from the lake and cooled off the hot spots . Darrel was very happy to see Bob and me and he was especially happy when we fired up the pumps and doused the fire lines.

Bob Lesmeister on the evening fire line on Cooper Mountain Fire.

The next morning, Sim had Bob and I flown down to Chelan so we could augment local fire crews. The storm had started fires all over the Chelan District and Sim and Ed Armbruster were having difficulty keeping up with

84

them. Bob took a crew to the Cooper Mtn.(on the North side of Lake Chelan) fire where he had his hands full with a lightning caused blaze that almost got out of control. At the same time I was assigned to a fire started by lightning above Twenty-Five Mile Creek on the South

Jim Higgins on the Twenty-Five Mile Creek Fire.

side of the lake. Jim Higgins, Doug Bowie and I put out that fire very quickly.

Two days later, John Ward, Roger Stafford (just returned from Stehekin) and I were sent up to the Cooper Mtn. Fire to assist Bob and his crew. John and Roger had remained at the Hunt's Bluff fire and mopped up after Bob and I were sent down lake. But, Sim needed them for fire control work out of the Chelan Ranger Station and he had brought them home the night before. After two more days mopping up at Cooper Mtn., all of the recently caused fires were under control and Forest Service managers breathed a collective sigh of relief. It was a good thing as most of us had to return to college to begin fall classes.

There was a bit of a downer for us at the close of that season as bonds of friendship had been forged over the summer in the mountains and on the fire lines. We all looked forward to working together again and we speculated about where we would end up the following summer. Rumor had it that Bob, John, Roger and I would all work together on a helicopter borne (it was called "Helitack", short for helicopter attack) fire suppression crew which was a relatively new idea at the time. All of us were very enthusiastic and excited about the prospect of being a part of that concept.

The author uses a Pulaski to point out the effect of the lighning strike on a Yellow Pine which caused the Twenty-Five Mile Creek Fire.

Ed Pulaski's contribution to wildland fire fighters.

The tool in the author's hand is a Pulaski, which has been used for nearly one hundred years as one of the basic fire fighting tools of the U.S. Forest Service. It was invented by Edward Pulaski, the Forester who saved the lives of 40 men on the Fire of 1910. Pulaski was never reimbursed for the money he spent on medical bills for himself or his injured fire crew members despite appeals to Congress. Further, he was never given a patent for his invention seen above. **Note:** While the author appears wearing a T-shirt on this fire, it would not be allowed today. Modern fire fighters wear clothing made of fire resistant Nomex fabric on today's fire lines. The shirts are long-sleeved.

Chapter Fourteen:
Grade Creek Brush Camp

Despite the thrill of the prospective new job for the following year, I had a reason for apprehension at the beginning of this school year. When Bob and I were cleaning the trail at Swamp Creek, one of the letters left for me in the trail crew mail sack by Ray Courtney was from the Registrar at Washington State University. That letter made it very clear that I would have to prove my academic worth this semester-or else! At the time I was a little scared, and had no idea of how I was going to produce but, I was determined to succeed.

I sure wasn't looking forward to meeting the Reinstatement Board or hearing their conditions for my return, but I appeared on schedule and promised to get my academic standing back on track. Although my grades were poor I was allowed to reenroll on a probationary status.

Thanks to my girlfriend Betty, two helpful Fraternity brothers at Delta Tau Delta, and a lot of discipline, I achieved a 3.75 GPA carrying

18 semester hours. It became a great school year reinforced by continued academic success and I had no difficulty maintaining good grades from then on. I was again summoned by the Board, but this time for congratulations....and an admonishment for not having achieved similar results during my first two years of college.

The end of the school year found me breaking over the top of McNeil Canyon on my way home to Chelan and a much-anticipated summer of fighting fire. It was 1962 and Bob, John, Roger and I were, as rumored earlier, assigned to the same crew. We were all elated to learn that together, we were to constitute the first Helicopter Fire Suppression Crew at Chelan. We would be based at what came to be known as the "BD (brush disposal) Camp" where we would enjoy a bunkhouse, shower house and single-wide trailer which served as kitchen and supplemental bunkhouse for additional crew members and our boss. The latter was a nice fellow but he knew nothing of the work at hand and was not at home in the mountains.

The BD Camp was located up the Grade Creek Road above Manson, and it was situated near logging activities which provided us brush cleaning work between fires. The location was well suited for helicopter crew pick up and dispatch. However, it worked well in concept only, for there were very few fires that summer. We never boarded a helicopter at anytime during the season. But, the idea was put into expanded practice with great success in later years. In fact, Bob's younger brother Tar was one of the first members and a foreman of the first Helitack crew which was formed at Chelan in 1972. Kyle Engstrom of Chelan was another member and also an early foreman of this group.

These Helitack members had to undergo extremely vigorous conditioning and physical testing which approached similar standards required

The bunkhouse at the Brush Disposal (BD) Camp.
This building housed a crew of four but was large
enough to accomodate several more.

Showerhouse at the BD Camp.

John Ward (L) and Roger Stanford in a lighter moment reflecting the boredom of a summer of stacking brush.

of smokejumpers. They rappelled from helicopters to fight fire and distinguished themselves on many occasions.

For our crew, the summer of 1962 was frustrating and involved hours of boredom-cutting and stacking brush behind logging operations. This was not the glamorous work of fighting fire, but rather, it was a lesson in staying focused.

One very memorable event did occur while we were stationed at the BD camp. During the only severe thunderstorm of the summer, we were dispatched up the Grade Creek Road to look for "smokes" from lightning strikes in the late afternoon. Four of us piled into a green Forest Service panel van and headed up the road. Discretion prevents me from identifying the driver, but let it suffice to say that I sat on a rear bench, seat belt fastened securely and looking forward to a little action. Little did I know what was in store for us.

The Grade Creek Road traverses some high, open hillsides that descend a thousand feet to Lake Chelan in some places. In the area are remnants of an old log chute, or flume, that was constructed to move logs from the hillside down to the lake. For the most part, these logs travelled at the favor of gravity. Considering the steepness of the hillside, they must

Cumulus cloud passing over BD camp that built into a storm which produced several lightning-caused fires.

have reached incredible velocities on the way down to the lake. Essentially, they became missiles with limited guidance systems and they must have been quite a sight as they raced down the chute!

Up we went, passing a logging crew that was closing down for the day. Those in the two front seats had the best visibility and were looking for tell tale wisps of smoke as we drove along. We continued along uneventfully, except for two occasions on which the driver took his eyes off the road. It was the job of the passengers to look for fires, not the driver. But, he could not resist and off the road we went.

I am not exaggerating when I say that this action elicited several blunt comments from the passengers; all punctuated with colorful bits of profanity directed towards our now somewhat terrified driver. After all, he was in the best position to see where we were headed and, no doubt, was scared.

Bill Moody Photo

Night time lightning strike.

As a result, he became highly animated and went through all sorts of vigorous physical activity in an attempt to get us stopped. This including riding the brakes, downshifting, and so on, all to no avail. Meanwhile, we passengers knew we were all going to die and could do nothing about it other than to berate the driver.

FOUR-ELEVEN!

After what seemed an eternity we came to an abrupt stop. The van had assumed a very steep, nose down attitude, much the same as one of the logs in the flume on its' way to the lake. The two of us in the rear of the van were literally lying on our backs on the rear benches, hanging from the seat belts which now held us just under our armpits.

No one said a word. No one moved. I think we even stopped breathing as we didn't want to do anything to cause the van to move. Finally, the front seat passenger said "Faletto, I think it is safe to open the back door and climb out. Go for it and get help from that logging crew back down the road. And don't let the door slam behind you."

Because I was fighting gravity, I had a very hard time getting out of the seat belt. Opening the door was also quite a chore for the same reason. Meanwhile, the other passengers were not convinced that the van would remain where it stopped, and my movements seemed to upset them. But, despite their complaints, I was soon outside.

I found that we had hit the only rock on that hillside, and that is where we had stopped. I told the others they were safe and then I took off running to try and catch the logging crew before they left for the day. I was wearing my Whites, but I think I covered the mile or so back to the loggers in about four and one half minutes. I am sure I was still feeling the effects of the adrenalin rush caused by our mishap.

The loggers of course were puzzled to see me running down the road, waving and trying to catch their attention. They thought that our predicament was pretty funny and they howled with laughter when I told them what had happened. The logging foreman sent an operator and a D-6 Caterpillar with me aboard back up to rescue the van. When we got there, my compatriots were all standing on the road looking very serious. They'd had had time to assess the situation-as well as our good fortune. It was a long, long way down to the lake and the one thing that could have saved us — the rock — did!

The Cat skinner had chuckled all the way to the scene, but, when he looked over the side at the vehicle, he sobered considerably. Thanks to him, and his machine, we were back on the road in no time. Incredibly, there was not a scratch on the van and the under carriage was undamaged. The front bumper had a small dent, but it was not very noticeable. Thankfully, we had been going very slowly, and we didn't go much more than two to three vehicle lengths off of the road.

We didn't find any fires that evening and we were pretty quiet as we drove back to the BD camp.

Our boss said, "Well boys how did it go? Spot any fires?" No one said a word. We just shook our heads. It had been that kind of day.

Four-Eleven!

Chapter Fifteen:
The Last Summer on the Ground

We worked hard that summer, stacking brush and cleaning up behind the logging operations conducted nearby. The drudgery of it all was broken by visitors from the Chelan Ranger Station and the occasional build-up of cumulus clouds. The latter, of course brought the hint of lightning storms (and the possibility of overtime work on the fire lines) and the former gave us the chance to talk to a new face in camp. One of those visitors was Dick Swier, who was the Timber Sale Officer for the Chelan Ranger District. Dick was fun to have around because of his outgoing personality and positive outlook. And, he came by frequently because of the timber sale activity in the area.

For me, Dick added an interesting dimension to our conversations because he was a private pilot. As a young Air Force ROTC cadet destined for flight training, I jumped at any and all opportunities to talk about flying with someone who understood. Dick was very patient with all of my questions about flying and gave me much encouragement to pursue a career in aviation. Coincidentally, I ran into Dick at Felts Field in Spokane later that fall when I went there from Pullman to take my private pilot's exam.

As the summer of 1962 drew to a close, we who had been together for the past couple of summers decided that it would be a good idea to have an end- of- season party at a summer cabin on the lake. We knew we would not work together again as Forest Service employees and added that to the list of reasons to justify the party. And party we did. We water-skied, drank beer and ate hamburgers until late at night. We did have a couple of party crashers but, there were no fights-we didn't invite any smokejumpers- and, we didn't run out of beer. It was a pretty dull party by local standards! There was one motor cycle accident that resulted in cuts and bruises but, we had a lot of fun and no one suffered any long term damage.

The following morning — way too early the following morning — Bob and I were called to the Chelan Ranger Station for fire guard duty at Twenty-Five Mile Creek Guard Station. There was a threat of a late summer thunder storm with a high probability of lightning. It was Sunday and neither one of us had had enough sleep. Worse yet, we were both feeling the effects of too much fun the night before.

When we got to the guard station, our instructions from Sim were to hook up the trolley system that had been built to haul gravel from a large pile in the station parking lot. The system moved the gravel uphill to a long septic trench that had been carved into the rocky hillside above. Considering that it was a hot day and, that we were not in the best condition for this type of manual labor, it should be no surprise that we prayed for the few breaks we got. Finally, to our relief, we got a fire call and went up the Twenty-Five Mile Creek Road to put it out. It was a small fire, and with the help of a crew dispatched from Chelan, it was extinguished very quickly.

Source: Det# 905 A.F.R.O.T.C., Pullman, WA

R.O.T.C. Flight Program students in 1962. Author in center, kneeling.

Chapter Sixteen:
Aerial Observer/Pilot Duty

My junior year at WSU was a huge turning point in my life and very exciting to say the least. I was promoted rapidly in the U.S.A.F. Detachment #905 R.O.T.C. program and became the cadet Deputy Wing Commander. More importantly I was accepted into the Flight Instruction Program. After all, it had been my goal for many years to fly as an Air Force pilot.

I also became engaged to, and married, my girlfriend, Betty, in December of 1962. To top it all off, I received my Pilot's License in the spring of 1963. I had come a long way in a very short period of time, overcoming serious academic deficiencies and achieving substantial goals that I had set for myself.

Just after the school term ended I learned that I had been hired by Jack Fowler, Aviation Fire Control Officer for Region 6 as the Observer/ Pilot (GS-5) for the Forest Service out of the Aerial Fire Base at Pangborn

The U.S.F.S. Air Operations Base at Pangborn Field in Wenatchee, Washington, with the Wenairco PB4Y2 in the background.

Field in Wenatchee. Jack was a popular leader, well known in the fire suppression business.

My immediate boss at the fire base was George Carberry from Entiat, and he too was a special individual. George taught high school during the school year, and worked for the U.S. Forest Service in summer as manager of the Aerial Tanker Base at Pangborn. An added bonus was that Doug Bowie, who I had worked with in Chelan, was also assigned to the aerial fire suppression team under Carberry. Doug was responsible for air cargo operations, including preparation, packing and aerial delivery of food and supplies to smokejumpers and fire crews in the field. He continued with the USFS and retired after a 34 year career, 26 of which were spent

U.S. Forest Service Photo

Aerial view of base at Pangborn Field.

in fire suppression activities. In retrospect, the USFS entrusted substantial responsibility to relatively inexperienced young men and the coming summer tested all of us to the limit.

I was ecstatic at having been selected for the flying job. Working around me that summer were men who were near legends in the business. Bill "Red" Byers, Keith Bonner, Lyle Flick, Joe Madar, Herm Gallagher, Bob Conine and Willard Skoglun — who owned Columbia Skyways — all flew out of the Wenatchee base. Bonner was the resident Forest Service pilot flying the Forest Service T-34. Flick and Madar, pilot and copilot, flew the PB4Y2 and PV2 tankers stationed at the base and they, along with Gallagher, and Conine worked for Wenatchee Air Service. Byers owned and operated two B-26s that he flew up from Burns, Oregon to use on fires in the Wenatchee area, and on neighboring Ranger Districts.

These men were the best! They literally took me under their wings and taught me about the rigors of mountain flying. They all knew that I was

Forest Service T-34 lead plane with Fire Warehouse in background.

101

eventually going into the Air Force Pilot Training program and they went out of their way to help me learn.

To some degree, this was in their best interest as I served as copilot on the C-180 and C-172 for some of them. Therefore, they made sure I was capable of bringing them home safely if need be. Flick, Gallagher and Madar flew the tankers for Wenairco (Wenatchee Air) so I normally did not fly with them. But since Conine, with Wenairco, and Skoglun, with Columbia Skyways, flew fire patrol under contract with the Forest Service, I flew with one or both of them on almost a daily basis. From time to time, Gallagher and Madar did fly the Wenairco Cessna 180 as fill-in pilots and they too "signed off" my log book.

The Wenatchee Forest Service base from which we flew was established in 1961. The facility was built as a centralized fire retardant storage and delivery base as well as a warehouse for fire suppression supplies. Keystones of the operation were the 500 gallon mixing tank and two large 10,000 gallon storage tanks for Borate (white) and Bentonite (pink) fire retardant slurry. The base also featured three separate "pits" where aircraft were parked to take on loads of retardant pumped from the big tanks .

Periodically, these tanks had to be cleaned, and both Doug Bowie and I were assigned to accomplish the task. Getting inside them was necessary to get the job done, and that was not fun, I can assure you. It was hot and humid work, and it was easy to become claustrophobic while inside. We got into the tanks, worked as fast as we could and got out as quickly as possible.

Doug and I were also primarily responsible for mixing the the liquid retardant-or the "slurry" as it was called. We cut open a seemingly endless number of paper bags of Borate (borax salt) or Bentonite (aluminum silicate clay) and dumped them into the mixing tank. By adding water,

Borate and Bentonite fire retardants.

Retardant slurry becomes very heavy because the powder absorbs large amounts of water. It is sticky and easily adheres to most anything with which it comes in contact and that helps it smother fire. The Borate mixture weighs 10.4 lbs. per gallon and the Bentonite mix weighs about 9 lbs per gallon.

This weight issue is so significant that wings have separated from WWll vintage aircraft due to negative 'Gs' created when the load was dropped and the plane shot skyward. Years of stress caused by flying can result in metal fatigue, and some older, unmodified aircraft have not been able to tolerate the sudden and very forceful lift that follows the release of retardant. A tragic example occurred in July of 1960 when Wenairco's B-25 crashed on the Beaver Lake fire for this very reason. Pilot George Carey and Co-pilot J.C. Brehm perished in the accident.

Not only is the heavy retardant an issue for aircraft but it is a source of concern for those on the ground as well. Stories persist about firefighters being knocked down by the heavy retardant though I've never heard of any being killed or injured. Nevertheless, fire fighters are always warned to avoid being hit by the drops.

Borate was generally used to fight fire in timber and Bentonite on grass and sagebrush fires. Since Borate has a higher specific gravity, it was found to better penetrate forest canopies. Bentonite, on the other hand, is used as a fire suppressant rather than as a retardant. Because of this, it can be used on hot spots within a fire's perimeter that are potentially dangerous. The latter is superior in terms of cost comparison.

Borate is no longer allowed for use in fire fighting because it is toxic to animals and sterilizes soil. Replacement chemicals, such as ammonium polyphosphate with an attapulgite clay thickener, are less toxic and act as a fertilizer to aid plant growth after the fire has been put out. Generally, a red dye such as ferric oxide, is added to mark drop locations.

U.S. Forest Service Photo

U.S. Forest Service Photo

500 gallons were prepared at a time. The resultant mix was a thick, soupy compound.

The retardant mixing operation. Top: 500 gallon mixing tank with two 10,000 storage tanks for Borate and Bentonite. Above: Forklift with bags of Borate delivered for mixing of the retardant slurry. Below: Retardant loading pit with hose line on wheeled carts which rolled across the tarmac to reach the old bombers.

On a hot day, the dust which arose from emptying the bags coated everything including ourselves, and sometimes it made breathing difficult. But, the mixture, a thick soupy compound, was manageable once it was finished and placed in the storage containers. It was then easily pumped into the cavernous tanks in the bellies of the big World War II bombers which had been converted to fight fire.

U.S. Forest Service Photo

U.S. Forest Service Photo

Bombs away! A short history of aerial fire suppression and air cargo delivery.

Various types of WWII medium bombers (PV-2, B-25, PB4Y-2) converted to use for delivering fire retardant parked on the ramp in front of the U.S.F.S. Fire Warehouse.

According to a 1962 report written by J.K. Blair, Forest Supervisor for Region 6, some early testing which resulted in the aerial fire retardant methods of today, occurred in the Wenatchee National Forest in 1956. This effort was marked by drops of up to 60 gallons of water through nozzles mounted under the wings of a Super Cub on a "going fire". Blair went on to say that, when drops from the Super Cub proved successful, similarly-equipped Stearmans actively attacked fires on the Wenatchee during 1957 and 1958. These planes, which carried 150 gallons of water, had a very limited range of operation that was no further than 20 miles from the base in East Wenatchee. Within this radius however, the Stearmans "were very effective." Beyond the radius, "their small gallonage capacity and their slow speed made their effectiveness questionable."

Blair's report also states that in the summer of 1958, "a local company (Wenairco) purchased a B-25 bomber and installed in it a 1000 gallon tank. During 1959, both the Stearman and the larger bomber were used on fires." The report goes on to say that "the larger load and greater speed made the B-25 a much more effective plane to use in the (continued on Page 107)

U.S. Forest Service Photo

Warehouse operations.

Another extremely vital facet of the fire suppression triad (including retardant activity, and air operations) was the warehouse. This 6,500 sq. ft. facility at Pangborn field housed hundreds and hundreds of fire- fighting tools including Pulaskis, shovels, axes, grub hoes, hoses, pumps, canteens, pack boards, disposable sleeping bags, containers, packing materials and parachutes.

All of us came to be very proficient in packing cargo chutes and related gear for aerial delivery to fire crews. Many

U.S. Forest Service Photo

Tool cache inside the Fire Warehouse.

(from Page 105) suppression of fires." These developments, coupled with the need for a larger, Forest Service-owned facility and a longer runway, resulted in the establishment of the Aerial Fire Base at Pangborn Field in 1961.

There is evidence that the first forestry-related air cargo drops were made as early as 1929. David Godwin, Assistant Chief of Fire Control, Washington Office, and a proponent of aerial fire control operations, was in charge of an experimental project in 1938 which tested the effectiveness of dropping retardant on fires. It was concluded that this method was not effective and the funds were shifted to another project which was tasked to develop a "safe and practical method of dropping men by parachute to fight forest fires," (*Spittin' in the Wind*, Moody and Longley.) That project landed squarely in the Chelan National Forest at Winthrop, Washington and became the forerunner of modern day smokejumping.

Milestones mentioned in the Blair report highlight the fact that much of the early history of aerial fire suppression operations took place in the Chelan and Wenatchee National Forests. The "air minded" Forest Service innovators from this area perfected many of the techniques used today including not only retardant drops, but use of "lead planes," fire patrol and air cargo delivery.

Lead planes, according to Blair, are absolutely vital when "more than two retardant planes are used on a fire" because they help to minimize danger due to congestion. Since fire conditions often change between trips to reload retardant, the pilot of the lead plane, which remains loitering over the fire, is aware of this and can communicate new priorities to the bombers. Further, use of lead planes -sometimes referred to as "bird dogs"- saves time by identifying drop areas picked out in advance. It also provides a vital safety element by alerting ground crews to safety considerations.

It is interesting to note that some of today's fire suppression aircraft carry far greater loads at much higher speeds than the old medium bombers first used to attack fires. One such aircraft is Evergreen Airline's Supertanker, a converted Boeing 747 that can carry monstrous loads of retardant up to 24,000 gallons – or 120 tons – at speeds in excess of 350mph.

U.S. Forest Service Photo

Wenairco B-25 that was converted to carry retardant in 1958. This plane was probably the same one that was lost in 1960 on the Beaver Lake Fire.

of the supplies, including hot meals cooked and packed just two-three hours before delivery, were flown to hungry smokejumpers, hot shot crews and local fire fighters in the Cessna 180 with the passenger door removed. More often though, this cargo was delivered in the old Pilgrim, a single engine, high wing, fabric covered aircraft that cruised at about 80 mph. It looked much like a Ford Tri-Motor, with only one engine. Smokejumpers and "cargo kickers"- men like Doug Bowie who pushed supplies out the door-loved this old, slow and very forgivable airplane as it was a comfortable delivery platform from which to work.

We took the job of packing cargo chutes very seriously. George Carberry taught us to be meticulous and careful with each fold of the chute and clip of rubber bands around the "S" folded shroud lines. After hours and hours of hot, smoky and dusty work on a fire, no one enjoys scraping his or her evening meal from the inside of a smashed cargo container that resulted from a "streamer." A streamer is a parachute which fails to open and slams into the ground at a high rate of speed. It tends to be rough on the contents.

We were equally careful in aligning the actual drops. However, I do recall one on a fire in the Entiat valley which did not work out well. It was there that I dropped a cargo pack that drifted onto the very top of the only tall tree in the area. It was an evening meal delivery, and I am sure I was not popular with that fire crew, especially the young man who had to climb the tree and retrieve the parachute which held up his dinner.

An added incentive for diligent and professional work was that many of those fire fighters — especially smokejumpers — transited our Wenatchee facility on their way home after the fire was out. None of us were the least bit interested in being confronted by a dirty, exhausted, sleep-deprived fire fighter who was unhappy about equipment or meal deliveries.

The remaining area of activity at the base was Air Operations. This included retardant delivery and aerial observation, the latter of which was my area of responsibility. Retardant delivery was a matter of coordination between George Carberry and Jack Fowler. They also coordinated with contract companies such as Wenairco and Byers, arranging aerial delivery as needed in response to requests from area fire bosses. These requests moved up the chain of command from District to National Forest Headquarters.

I flew with Columbia Air Service and Wenairco plus a few times with Keith Bonner in the Forest Service owned T-34. The two companies had contracts with theForest Service for fire patrol. It was our job to spot fires, report them and coordinate air operations while over an active fire. We also dropped supplies and food to fire fighters.

The routes we flew were pre-arranged so that we, and those we worked with, would know where we were in general terms. The most common route took us from Pangborn Field in East Wenatchee across the Columbia River and up to what is now Mission Ridge Ski Area, then west along the Mission Ridge, then over to the Stuart Range, up to Lake Wenatchee and on over to the head of the Entiat valley and home again. This was approximately a two and one- half to three hour flight in a Cessna 180. Sometimes, our flight time could be stretched a little longer, as the aircraft had a variable pitch prop. That feature allowed us to extend our range by altering propeller pitch which decreased our fuel consumption. On occasion that summer, we flew more than one mission a day due to excessive thunderstorm activity. By regulation, we were not to exceed eight hours per day as aircrew members.

When we did encounter a fire, it was my job to pinpoint the fire's exact location by determining Range, Township, section and quarter section. I then made the well known, in Forest Service circles, radio call which had an electrifying effect on all who heard it. "Wenatchee Base, this is Y10 Patrol Plane. Four-eleven." "Roger Y10 Patrol Plane, this is Wenatchee Base. Copy your four-eleven. Go ahead." I would then relay the coordinates and standby for further instructions.

Sometimes, I was instructed to loiter in the area and await the arrival of smokejumpers or retardant aircraft. At other times we were asked to remain in the area for ground crews to arrive so that I could help guide them to the fire and provide further support as necessary. In every case, the situation was different due to size of the event, the type of response and so on. It was always exciting, and it was always a time for concentration, situation awareness and precision. It was especially interesting when more than one aircraft-spotter, smokejumper and retardant for example-circled a fire in the mountains at same time. And when that happened, there was ample reason for being extremely careful in order to avoid mid air collisions.

U.S. Forest Service Photo

Forest Service Cessna 180 like the one flown by the author on fire patrol.

Chapter Seventeen
Air Orientation

My first flight from Pangborn Field on fire patrol was with Jack Fowler in the right seat and Willard Skoglun in the left. As mentioned earlier, Willard owned Columbia Skyways and he had a contract for patrol activity that summer with the Forest Service. Jack was the Fire Control Officer at the Wenatchee Forest Office and he had firm and specific ideas about aerial fire reconnaissance. The patrol route that I described in the previous chapter was defined by him and we flew it that day.

I was in the back seat and the aircraft Willard flew was a Cessna 172. It lacked the stronger performance characteristics of the Cessna 180 which was our preferred "ship" for mountain flying, but it was comfortable and reliable. As we climbed up towards Mission Ridge I was able to look down on what was then known as the Squilchuck Ski Area as well as the nearby Boy Scout Camp where I had spent a week in each of 3 earlier summers as a young Scout. To this day, I value those early years as a Cub Scout, Boy

Author on fire patrol over the Entiat Valley.

Scout, Explorer and member of the Brotherhood of the Order of the Arrow. The valuable lessons I learned from scouting will remain with me for the rest of my life.

I was startled back to reality when I heard Fowler call Beehive Lookout and report our progress over the flight route. It became obvious that this first flight was really a training flight scheduled primarily for my benefit and Jack was a good teacher.

We flew west along Mission Ridge and then turned southwest towards the magnificent Stuart Range. The Stuarts are a series of rocky peaks that thrust dramatically skyward, much like the Grand Tetons in Wyoming. In fact, the Stuarts even resemble the Tetons from certain angles. They are breathtaking in their beauty, especially from a small airplane that dances along their flanks with light updrafts as flying partners on a warm summer day.

From the Stuarts, Jack and Willard guided us to the northwest and Lake Wenatchee. We flew on, with Jack making sure that I saw the auxiliary landing strips along our route. The fields at Leavenworth and Lake Wenatchee were the only ones that afforded comfortable width and distance, but any place that we could put the aircraft down safely was always a welcome sight while flying in these mountains. We identified several of the latter on various ridges, meadows and mountain slopes along our routes. Eventually, we turned down the Entiat Valley, intersected the Columbia River, and flew on home to Pangborn Field in East Wenatchee.

Flying too close to the edges of the air.

Above the Boy Scout camp I attended and scattered under the rim of a rocky outcropping, lay the remains of a WW 11 era B-24 that crashed there while on a training mission in the early 1940s. I had heard about it many times at Scout camp and now saw it as a symbol of a mistake that perhaps, could have been avoided. I made a mental note on that morning of my first training flight about flying "too close to the edges of the air" as early aviators were fond of saying. To do so could have disastrous results, as evidenced by the wreckage below.

This orientation flight was an unforgettable experience that left me on "information overload." I heard rapid-fire comments from the front seats about landmarks, ridgetops that bred dangerous downdrafts, potential fire traps and especially, usable landing spots. On top of trying to assimilate all of that information, I tried hard to pay close attention to the handling characteristics of the Cessna 172. Willard Skoglun was an experienced and highly skilled pilot who was very smooth in his movements. He was always way ahead of his airplane at all times. By that I mean that he anticipated flight movements well in advance which is crucial in any type of flying but especially important in the mountains. I would learn a lot more about mountain flying when I was able to fly the plane under his supervision as well as others.

After we landed, I felt like I had already put in a good days work. Listening to my two mentors and experiencing the intense concentration that was involved had made me tired. I would later learn just how fatigued one could feel after a day of flying, especially after the fire season started.

Author's log book.
Note signatures of
Keith Bonner, Bob
Conine and Herm
Gallagher certifying
dual time.

Chapter Eighteen:
Air Operations from Pangborn Field

A fter three more orientation/patrol flights, Willard was confident enough in my ability to fly the airplane that he gave me the opportunity to sit in the left, or pilot's seat. I was exhilarated as I taxied the Cessna 172 to runway 29 at Pangborn Field. Willard sat in the right seat. Our agreement was that I would fly until we spotted a fire, whereupon he would take the controls and I would work the fire as the Forest Service Aerial Observer. In that way, I could begin to log solo flying time and gain more experience. He, on the other hand, could relax or catch a cat nap. In actuality, he never slept and he knew exactly what was going on at all times.

In the today's world of Forest Service air operations, I would not be allowed to assume any pilot duties or even touch the controls. Further, the C-172 would not be allowed to operate as a patrol plane as it does not meet today's horsepower requirements specified by the Forest Service. However, in 1963 existing circumstances were very beneficial to me in

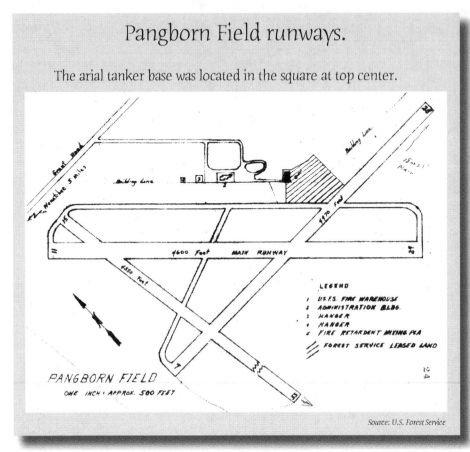

Pangborn Field runways.

The arial tanker base was located in the square at top center.

Source: U.S. Forest Service

gaining experience. Especially so when Willard, who was supposedly nap-ping, would shut off a fuel flow valve causing the engine to quit and me to go through a brief, but very focused effort to figure out why.

Exercises like this one were favorites of the older, experienced men I flew with and, in short, they made me a better mountain pilot. On every occasion, challenges like this caused me to immediately note our location, altitude, possible landing sites and so on. Each of those things were taken into consideration while I was trying to figure out why the airplane's engine had ceased operating. Flying is a game of situation awareness, and with mountain flying, situation awareness must be absolutely constant.

It was a bright, beautiful morning in early July of 1963 and I was elated to be where I was. I was confident about handling the airplane and confident in my ability to do the job that I was hired for. After reaching the end of the taxi way, I stopped short of the active runway and ran the engine up, checking the "mag's" and watching the instruments to make sure everything was running smoothly. Willard nodded approval. Satisfied that we were ready, I called Wenatchee tower for clearance to take off and visually cleared for any approaching aircraft. I then "cranked in" flaps and turned N6916X onto the "active" and opened the throttle.

Down the runway we went-on our way to complete a routine fire patrol flight. Fifty, 60 then 80 miles per hour, and then, just before lift off, there was a loud "bang" and the aircraft pulled to the right. At a point where I considered it too late to abort the flight, I eased back on the yoke and the plane lifted off the runway. I looked at Willard and he just shrugged and offered a puzzled look. He looked out the window and could see nothing wrong on his side of the plane. Our instruments gave us no indication of trouble and the airplane was flying just fine. So, I called the tower and asked permission for a "flyby" which would allow them to conduct a visual inspection. I explained that we had, apparently, hit something on the runway. The tower agreed and the flyby revealed nothing that appeared to be out of order. After discussing options with Willard, we agreed there was no reason to cancel our patrol flight. Whatever had gone wrong would probably remain unchanged and we would wait until we finished the business at hand to learn what it was.

The flight took us up the usual route over Mission Ridge, on to the Icicle River, up past Lake Wenatchee to the headwaters of the Entiat and home again. It was a gorgeous day in the mountains and the beauty of the

FOUR-ELEVEN!

Stuart Range and the high Cascades in the Glacier Peak Wilderness Area were breathtaking. Snow was melting in the high country and summer thunderstorm activity was yet to come. For now, we reveled in the incredible mountain vistas that marked our route.

When we reached Ardenvoir, a small town part way up the Entiat Valley, we turned in a southeasterly direction towards our home field. Once over the mountains on the south side of the valley, the drier country on the east side of the Columbia River came into view. And with that, I was jolted back into reality with the thought that we had a potential problem when we landed the airplane. Being the dutiful student that I was, I offered control of the plane back to Willard. He gave me a rather incredulous look, folded his arms and said, "Hey, you got us into this, you can get us out of it! You land the airplane."

Frankly, I had not expected that response but it sure got my attention. I realized he meant every word he said. He had told me in no uncertain terms that this was a situation that I would have to handle. At five miles out, I called Wenatchee Tower and requested a Precautionary Landing -no fire or crash rescue trucks-but a "just in case" advisory. We did another flyby which did not reveal any damage and circled back into the downwind and final approach legs of the landing pattern.

Suspecting something was wrong with the right main wheel, I touched down on the left main gear, allowing the aircraft to slow down. I kept it rolling on the left wheel and then added the nose wheel until the airplane settled naturally onto the right wheel as well. That is when the fun began. The airplane immediately pulled hard right. Tower advised smoke coming from the gear and I pulled the aircraft off the runway at the first exit and then into the sand between the taxiway and the main runway. Dust flew and the plane stopped quickly. At that point, Mr.

Skoglun and I made a rather hasty departure from the cockpit to be sure we were away from any possible danger.

As it turned out, there was no fire. There was just smoke, which stopped very quickly. On inspection, we found that the wheel faring on the passenger side of the airplane had hit an object -which was never found or identified- on the runway and fractured. A torn, jagged piece of the fiberglass faring had been pushed back into the wheel, which peeled it further back as it rotated forward. Both the tire and wheel were destroyed along with the faring.

I suppose I should have been scared, but I recall feeling fairly calm about the incident. In retrospect, I suppose what little training I had, had counted for a whole lot more than I could have expected. Add to that to Willard's quiet demeanor and a whole lot of luck and we got safely through a challenging situation. The part I remember best about the event is that, as we walked away from the airplane, Willard put his hand on my shoulder and said "Good job." N6916X was flying again a few days later.

Bill "Red" Byers on top of his B-26 during a period of high activity during the Bird Creek Fire. Keith Bonner is at the controls of the T-34 taxiing out of the Fire Base for takeoff.

Chapter Nineteen:
"Four Eleven!"

'W'enatchee Base, this is Y-10 Patrol plane, Four Eleven !"
Willard and I were again on patrol and headed down the valley
toward Entiat when we spotted a plume of smoke to the northeast near
Navarre Coulee. Navarre is a little pass that runs between the Columbia
River and Lake Chelan. Upon investigation, we located a fire in the vicin-
ity of the Johnson and Bird Creek drainages.

The corner of the map I was using had been torn, and did not cover
the area in question, so I called the lookout on Chelan Butte for assistance
with the coordinates. That gentleman had a reputation for being surly
and unresponsive to radio calls and he refused to answer, or so I thought.
Frustrated, I tried to radio the Entiat Ranger Station to alert them of the
fire. After repeated calls, which met with no response, it became evident
that my radio was not working. So, I did the only thing I could think of to
solve the problem. I drew a map depicting the fire location and dropped

it on the front lawn of the ranger station in an aerial delivery pouch. Our low approach, along with the message pouch trailing a bright yellow streamer, got their attention. In a very short time we saw two fire crew vehicles leave the station and turn up Highway 97 towards the Navarre Coulee Road.

We then returned to the fire and circled, waiting for their arrival. What we didn't know was that another Forest Service vehicle from the Entiat District had been in the area and the two men inside had also spotted the fire. They had started hiking towards it with tools in hand, ready to begin building a fire line. Since we did not have a working radio, we knew we could not contribute much to the effort and departed for our base in East Wenatchee.

Within two hours of landing, our radio was repaired — it was the antenna on the aircraft that was bad — and we flew back to what was now called the "Bird Creek Fire." While the Entiat Forest Service crews hit that fire very quickly, winds drove it across their lines and into extremely dry cheat grass, sagebrush and Lodgepole pine growth. There was nothing they could do to stop it from the ground. Therefore, aerial tankers were called in and their precision drops stopped the fire in several places. This allowed ground crews to quickly build more effective fire lines and begin the containment effort. But, the desired end result would take several more days of hot, grueling work by what had grown to a group of approximately 20 fire fighters.

Meanwhile, the Aerial Fire Suppression Base at Pangborn Field had become a hub of activity to support the fire suppression effort. Aerial tankers, loaded with Borate or Bentonite stood by ready to respond at a moment's notice. The hard-earned gains of the fire fighters on the ground were not about to be surrendered to another gust of wind.

Crews had to be fed and resupplied. Hot meals were prepared in a Wenatchee restaurant, packed in specially designed meal containers mated to parachutes, and dropped to hungry fire crews. Joe Madar was the pilot on most of those missions and Doug Bowie was the "Cargo Kicker". They flew in the single engine Pilgrim, carrying food and water as well as fire fighting equipment. They were loved by the ground crews.

Bill Moody Photo

"Paracargo" drop of meals and fire fighting tools to fire fighters similar to drops on the Bird Creek Fire.

On an equipment drop, Doug lost his glasses out the door of the aircraft as they flew over the fire lines. When he returned to base, he mentioned the loss but, we were all working so hard to support the fire crews, that no one paid much attention. There was little time for sympathy. Doug himself was so busy that he just kept flying and dropping supplies. There wasn't even time to refill the prescription for his glasses.

Three days later, after the Bird Creek Fire had finally been contained, four smokejumpers from the North Cascades Smokejumper Base were brought to our base in Wenatchee where a plane would pick them up and return them to Winthrop. They had just come off the Bird Creek Fire and they were dirty and tired and they were looking forward to a hot shower.

One of them said, "Some guy from Entiat found a pair of glasses hanging on a sagebrush near the fire line up at Bird Creek. Know anybody

SPECS FOUND...UNBROKEN — Doug Bowie, East Wenatchee, looks at his undamaged glasses which survived a 250-foot drop from an airplane and a raging forest fire.—Daily World Photo.

Doug Bowie examining his glasses after they were recovered on the Bird Creek Fire.

that might have lost them?" Sure enough, they turned out to be Doug's. A few days later, a reporter from the Wenatchee Daily World interviewed Doug about the incident. The resulting photo and news article earned Doug a lot of notoriety among Forest Service personnel that summer.

As crews continued to mop up, we started the job of assembling and sorting the equipment returned from the fire. Those items that were serviceable were cleaned and returned to inventory. Tools that were broken or damaged were taken to the dump and burned. We were extremely careful and protective of returned cargo chutes as they were so expensive and vital to the fire support mission. We accomplished only the simplest of minor repairs for them. Otherwise, we returned repairable chutes to the smokejumper base at Winthrop where the real professionals returned them to service.

Chapter Twenty
The Fires of August

August 2nd, 1963 was the day of the Seattle Seafair and Gold Cup hydroplane races. Most of us who worked at the Wenatchee facility were aviators or aviation oriented and, since the hydroplanes used Allison aircraft engines, we were race fans too. So, when we had to work that Saturday, we welcomed the fact that we would be close to a television set in the warehouse crew lounge where we could watch the races. We shared opinions on whether the winner would be Hawaii Kai III, driven by Norm Evans of Chelan or Miss Thriftway, driven by Bill Muncey of Seattle.

Thunderstorms were predicted and that is why it was necessary for us to work overtime that day. Around 10 a.m., during our morning break, we turned on the TV set and, briefly watched one of the first heats. Thunderstorms began building over Seattle's Lake Washington where the race was being held and flashes of lightning were clearly evident on the

TV screen. That storm became so violent that even the television commentators began to note the deteriorating weather conditions.

Keith Bonner said, "We'll be flying before the afternoon is over." Sure enough, the sound of thunder rumbled around the building by mid afternoon as the storm rolled over the Cascades and into the Wenatchee National Forest. Keith and I — in the back seat — went up in the T-34. We flew a relatively short fire patrol towards Leavenworth, then over to and down the Entiat and back to Pangborn Field. We did not spot any fires on that flight but heard Forest Service lookouts in two locations report "Four- Eleven." In some cases, smokejumpers were dispatched to stop more aggressive fires started by lightning strikes that afternoon but we did not, as yet, have fires to deal with in our area. Eventually, we returned to base and helped close down operations for the night.

The next day, all hell broke loose as fires were reported in several locations. On top of that, more thunderstorms were predicted for the coming week. By Monday, most all of us were airborne and flying several hours a day. Ground crews and smokejumpers were taxed to the limit as they moved from one fire to the next. We were involved in a classic "merry-go-round" — constant fire suppression activity going from one fire to the next.

Joe Madar and Doug Bowie loaded food for smokejumpers who were fighting a fire on Ibex Creek in the Icicle River drainage near Leavenworth. They took off in the Pilgrim which, as mentioned earlier, was a fabric covered airplane. Bob Conine and I went up in Wenairco's metal covered Super Cub around the same time to record lightning strikes for a study directed by Forest Service headquarters in Washington D. C. The idea was to note not only location of the strikes, but time and dates as well. The weather that blew in that afternoon produced hail and high winds as well as thunder and lightning.

Bill Moody Photo

This old Pilgrim dropped many smokejumpers and large amounts of cargo during her years of service to the Forest Service. This is the same plane that Joe Maddux and Doug Bowie flew into the hail storm which shredded the fabric on the wings.

The little Super Cub was thrown every which way in the storm and we continually went from straight and level to upside down, sideways and to other unusual attitudes as well.

Meanwhile, Bowie and Maddux were experiencing their own special set of events. They had been unable to locate the jumpers and the storm was worsening. Hail began to pierce the fabric of the Pilgrim and was bouncing on the floor of the cargo compartment where Doug was sitting. The radio fairly crackled with the sound of electricity produced by lightning as Doug told Joe about the hail. Shortly thereafter, Doug was heard to tell him that "fabric was beginning to tear off the starboard wing" as hail had also begun to puncture the wing fabric. According to an

129

unverified account of the story, Doug was then heard to say, "Do ya think I oughta jump, Joe?"

The unflappable Madar, in his classic drawl replied, "Don't you dare jump, Bowie. We only got one parachute."

Joe landed the old girl back in Wenatchee about 45 minutes later and she was a sight to behold. Fabric had torn loose in strips and trailed from the wings, flapping in the slip stream like handkerchiefs on a clothesline. The fuselage was peppered with holes and looked like it had been hit by a shotgun blast. The two crew members also looked a bit the worse for wear. The stress of riding in an airplane which was close to losing its ability to fly because of the fabric tears, caused the two of them to be extremely focused. Most of us thought the whole situation was pretty funny, but the two of them failed to see any humor whatsoever in the incident.

After about two hours work, and several rolls of duct tape — which the mechanic called "100 Mile An Hour Tape" — Wenairco had the Pilgrim ready to fly again. The two intrepid airmen took off, found the jumpers at Ibex Creek and delivered their cargo.

The work that we did plotting the lightning strikes was inconclusive. Fires started anywhere from within a few hours up to eleven days after the time of the strikes. In some cases though, crews were able to take advantage of the advanced notification and put out fires which started close to roads and which were easily accessible. In this way, some larger fires were prevented, so perhaps the "bumpy" ride was worth it?

Later in the week, Bob Conine and I were in the C-180 on the down wind leg of the traffic pattern at Wenatchee when we saw a large, twin engine aircraft on an unapproved, straight-in approach. It was coming right at us. The tower waived him off with a radio call and he circled and landed just after we did. The pilot was Bill "Red" Byers and his aircraft was a B-26 converted to carry and drop fire retardant.

Red was a real character who had flown bombers as an Air Force pilot in the Korean War. He also had been a trucker carrying explosives on Interstate 5 between Portland and Los Angeles. He told a newspaper reporter in an interview for The Wenatchee Daily World that he had hauled more explosives in his truck than he ever did in a bomber in Korea. When I met him he had at least one more B-26 and he was completely dedicated to the business of aerial fire fighting.

Wenairco had already based their PB4Y2-the Navy version of the Air Force B-24-at Wenatchee and, the addition of Byers' B-26 added much needed capability to our effort. It provided the Forest Service with a more economical means to deliver retardant to suppress smaller fires.

Byers flew several retardant missions out of Wenatchee during the rest of that week and into the next. While returning from one such flight, a hydraulic line, that ran through the aircraft ruptured and sprayed hydraulic fluid into the cockpit and onto the windscreen. Red was soaked in the smelly liquid. It was a minor miracle that he was able to land his plane as he had great difficulty seeing ahead. Apparently, he used his shirt as a rag to clean the interior windscreen and he landed safely.

For some reason, Red did not have a change of clothes. Fortunately, Doug Bowie was able to loan him a pair of pants and a shirt. With dry clothes and his plane repaired and re-loaded, Red took off to suppress another fire shortly thereafter.

He was always friendly and helpful, and he tried to talk me out of going into the Air Force, stating that my real future in flying was with helicopters. He kept telling me that I should try to get on with his friend Del Smith, a well-known Oregon helicopter pilot who eventually started

Bill Moody Photo

Evergreen International Airlines' 747 Supertanker.

Evergreen International Airlines. Coincidentally, I worked for Evergreen a few years after retiring from the Air Force and met Mr. Smith on more than one occasion. Recently, Evergreen converted one of its Boeing 747s into a fire suppression tanker which has already proven to be of value against fires in California last year. As a matter of interest, Bill Moody, former manager of the North Cascade Smokejumper Base in Winthrop, has worked on the project as a technical consultant.

Byers continued flying in support of Forest Service air attack operations for many years. Sometime in the mid 60s, Red crash-landed one of his B-26s in a farmer's wheat field somewhere in central Oregon. His aircraft was on fire when he touched down. The landing was hard and he bumped his head but, Red was wearing a helmet — he was one of the few pilots who did so on a regular basis — and, I am told, the helmet probably saved his life. According to the farmer who saw the crash, Byers ran out of his burning plane almost before it stopped and, he was moving faster than the airplane when it landed.

Lyle Flick, pilot, and Joe Madar, copilot flew the B-24 on several missions during the next fifteen days. The B-24 is much bigger than the B-26 and carried a much larger amount of fire retardant. It was a highly effective delivery platform and its payload tended to "lay a fire down" when it hit the ground. Fire fighters were always glad to see it coming because it was so effective. They also got out of the way in order to miss being hit by the retardant.

Bob Lesmeister Photo

Boulder Butte Lookout above Lake Chelan was manned by Bob Lesmeister when he spent a night there during a particularly violent thunder storm.

Chapter Twenty-One
The End of Summer

The storm caused many fires during the month of August and we flew numerous fire patrol missions. Once, we were asked by Ed Armbruster at the Chelan Ranger Station to divert from the upper Entiat drainage and fly a patrol from Meadow Creek on the north side of the lake and down to the Grade Creek area.

Several small fires had been caused by lightning strikes in the Chelan District although we did not find any on this particular mission. But, as we flew near Surprise Lake, the lookout on Boulder Butte, a station which had not been manned in twenty years, could be heard repeatedly trying to reach Chelan. "KOE 550 this is Boulder Butte, come in please."

There was no mistaking that voice. It was my former trail crew partner from the summer before, Bob Lesmeister.

Boulder Butte Lookout is located up Purple Creek above Stehekin and is difficult to reach because it sits very high on a rocky peak. Bob had been sent up there with a radio and limited supplies as a result of the storm. He'd had a busy time establishing himself as the resident lookout and in maintaining radio contact. For some reason, the dispatcher at Chelan could not hear him. So, I called Bob and after brief "hellos," I relayed his message.

Without benefit of an Osborne fire-finder table, and with only a compass, map and radio, he was able to only relay very basic information when he spotted a fire. Since the lookout had not been manned for so many years, it was in disrepair and Bob had to rewire the lightning rods. He made other repairs as well. During the height of the storm he sat on the bed with glass insulators on all four legs. Lightning flashed everywhere and the sky was illuminated as if it were the middle of the day. He later told me that he had heard the "hiss of oxygen sizzling from the heat of lightning as it formed ozone." Bob also mentioned that he could smell it. Since he was a chemistry major, as well as a highly experienced fire guard, I have no reason to doubt him.

Turning towards Twenty-Five Mile Creek, we flew along Slide Ridge headed for Navarre Coulee and the Columbia River. As we flew along another radio call to the Chelan Ranger Station crackled over the airways reporting a fire that had been contained. It was David Hale, the man who was the foreman of the first brush crew that I worked on during my first summer with the Forest Service. I called him and said hello, and he invited us to stop by for a cold bottle of his root beer. Since we had been flying for about two and one half hours, Conine and I would have loved to have been able to accept that invitation.

Our flight took us down the Columbia on the Entiat side of the river, and, as we drew closer to Wenatchee, I spotted smoke in the distance to the west. Turning towards the blue curl, that spiraled up from a thick stand of emerald green pines, we confirmed that it was an unreported blaze. Loitering overhead, we plotted the location and I called a 4-11 to Wenatchee for what came to be known as the "Tyee Fire." Coincidentally, there was an aircraft in the area with two smokejumpers on board. Within twenty minutes, the two jumpers went out the door and onto the grassy hillside below the fire. It was a classic case of enforcing the Forest Service policy of quick response in action!

Chumstick Fire. Note the heavy timber and underbrush that posed a threat to the crew that was hiking to this fire.

As we circled the site, I heard the lookout on Sugar Loaf talking to the lookout at Tyee. He said that he had not seen the fire before I reported it. He went on to tell Tyee that he was "amazed" at how closely I had come to identifying its location while, "bouncing around the sky," as he put it. "That guy nailed its location under one quarter of a mile," he said.

Lookouts were able to almost pinpoint a fire by utilizing the more stable Osborne fire-finder table located in the center of their little buildings. It had a sighting apparatus similar to a gun sight that allowed the lookout to line up the fire and then determine azimuth readings with the circular ring around the perimeter.

Calculating the location of a fire from an airplane is not all that difficult, but it's just not as precise as is making the calculation from a lookout. But, if one gets the calculation reasonably close, the ground crew, smokejumpers or retardant aircraft are generally able to see the smoke and locate the source.

A PV-2 drops retardant on the Chumstick Fire. (Note: the cable extending from the top of this picture and the one on Page 137 is the airplane's antenna.)

A few days later, Bob Conine and I were again up in the Cessna 180, this time to work a fire near Leavenworth called the Chumstick Fire. It had apparently been a "sleeper," a fire which was caused by lightning and had slumbered for a time before it burst into flame. Often, fuels on the forest floor that have been soaked with rain are so damp that fires smolder until conditions dry out the fuel and breezes fan the flames.

A Forest Service crew from Leavenworth was already on the fire line when we got there, and successfully slowing the fire's advance. Behind us came Flick and Madar in the PB4Y2 and we set up a drop run in coordination with the fire boss on the ground. The borate bomber fell in behind us. We then wagged our wings over the spot called out by the fire boss, and turned sharply away. The bomber flew straight ahead and dropped the retardant at the point that we had just marked. After two to three passes, stringing the borate along the front edge of the fire, the PB4Y2 returned to base for another load. They soon were back and ready again to make more drops and beat back the fire. In this way, the ground crews — more fire fighters had arrived by now — were able to contain the fire and begin mop up actions.

Since early reports of the fire had carried inaccurate information about its location, one crew that had been hiking in to find it was delayed by the roughness of the terrain and uncertainty of location. They had not been heard from for some time, and by chance, we spotted them as we made a wide circle around the fire. They were in a very dangerous spot about a half-mile out in front of the flames. The danger to them was posed by erratic winds that had been pushing the fire, and from dense brush and timber in the draws below and above them. After establishing radio contact with this group, we were able to relay a safe path of travel for them to avoid the leading edge of the fire. The incident was another example of the importance of good communications and coordination when fighting fire.

There have been several cases before and after in which fire fighters have found themselves in the wrong place at the wrong time and some have perished. For this reason, Forest Service personnel have constantly worked to insure that fire fighters are not only well-equipped, but well-informed and well-educated in the ways of dealing with fire in the mountains. Good communications continue to play a vital role in this effort.

Attitudes regarding early Forest Service policies have changed to some degree as evidenced by permitting accumulations of fuel in some forest areas to burn. In the past, man-caused "controlled burns" — other than logging slash abatement — were actively avoided and were the subject of criticism by environmental groups. Mother Nature herself took care of some of those dangerous areas that I saw in the Wenatchee National Forest in the early 1960s. Examples were the 1970 Entiat Burn where several lightning- caused fires (Shady Pass, Mitchell Creek, Gold Ridge, Burns Creek, Slide Ridge and Silver Basin) merged into one 122,000-acre-plus blaze. Over 8000 fire fighters were committed to stop that conflagration.

Another large blaze called the Fourth of July Fire occurred on the North side of Lake Chelan that same year. It was fueled by a large accumulation of logging slash.

What has not seemed to change is the love of forests and the high country by those who work for the Forest Service. Today's crew members are highly trained, physically tough young professionals, who are as much in love with the mountains as those who came before them. Today, women are also as much a part of the scene as are men.

It is difficult to explain the feelings that kept me coming back to work for the Forest Service summer after summer. Like my co-workers, I needed summer work to get through college but, we were all driven by the fact that we loved the work. Flying was the icing on the cake for me, and I still remember the thrill of soaring over the Stuart Peaks, making dead stick landings at the Lake Wenatchee air strip and cutting back the throttle while sneaking up on mountain goats asleep on a high, rocky ridge in the Cascades . Above all, I appreciate the friendships and camaraderie of the men with whom I shared those summer days.

Mid September found me saying goodbye at the Aerial Fire Base in Wenatchee as my summer drew to a close. I headed back to finish college in Pullman and to pursue a career in the Air Force.

Doug Bowie went on to spend a distinguished, 34-year career in fire suppression and watershed management for the Forest Service and he still does consulting work as a fire dispatcher. Jack Fowler retired from the Forest Service in 1980 after 32 years of fire and aviation management. Bill Moody has also retired from the Forest Service after 33 years at the North Cascades Smokejumper Base but he still does air attack consulting work. Bob Lesmeister completed a Masters Degree in chemistry at the University of

U.S. Forest Service Photo

Lookout Arne Jarvi with a Firefinder.

Montana and retired from Boeing Aircraft Company and also from the State of Washington, Dept. of Transportation. Bob's brother Tar is still involved with forest fire air attack as a contractor. Phil Clark retired from the Washington State Department of Natural Resources after serving 30-plus years in various jobs.

Today, trails in the Chelan District are still maintained by the U. S. Forest Service. Some are administered under contract by civilians. Trails in the North Cascades National Park are cared for by the National Park Service.

Pangborn Field is still the zone's fire cache for fire fighting tools and equipment. However, aerial operations — including fire patrol, lead plane, rappel, air attack and retardant operations — are now headquartered at the airport in Moses Lake, Washington.

Thankfully, much has been learned about forest stewardship over the years including safer and more effective methods of fire fighting, both on the ground and from the air. Clearly this knowledge is of great benefit. But, it has come at a great cost, and we all owe a debt of gratitude to those who paid the ultimate price.

*Bob Lesmeister (L) and the author at the junction of the
Domke Lake Trail on a return visit in 2009.*

Epilogue

There are many connections and coincidences that permeated my life as a result of my summers with the Forest Service. I knew the St. Luise family-Ernani was killed in 1929 on the Camas Fire-while growing up in Chelan. I worked with the brother of "Wag" Dodge who was the foreman of the Mann Gulch fire crew, on the Well's Dam project just before I went into the Air Force. I visited with Francis Lufkin and Bill Moody at the smokejumper base in Winthrop when we landed there to have our parachutes repacked in late summer of 1963. As mentioned earlier, my Dad and Francis were friends from their early days with the Forest Service.

Another coincidence happened in July of 1965 when I reported as a young Second Lieutenant to the Commander of the 759th Radar Squadron at Naselle Air Force Station, Washington. That commander turned out to be Major Hugo W. Schott, the very same fellow who, as a young officer, directed Army Air Corps radar and intercept operations against Japanese incendiary balloons out of Neah Bay, Washington 20 years earlier. Major Schott became a mentor and friend throughout my career in the Air Force.

An interesting aside is that, on at least one occasion in the early 1950s, a hunter carried a cannister into the office of the Chelan Police

Department. At the time, the UFO saga was a hot topic and perhaps he thought he had found some extra terrestrial hardware. Chief of Police Faletto knew instantly what it was and he wasted no time in telling the finder to get it out of his office. Of course, it was a remnant of one of the balloons from Honshu and it was probably still very dangerous.

I have had some interesting experiences in my life, but I am especially fond of those associated with the U.S. Forest Service. I have had fun reconnecting with several of the people mentioned herein, and that has made this an extremely rewarding endeavor.

Source: Bob Lesmeister

Bob and Sue Lesmeister at the Domke Complex Fire, 2007. Bob and Sue are the Hosts at the Lucerne Guard Station during summer months and worked as staff personnel on the fire. Their shirts and pants are made of Nomex, a fire resistant fabric. Both carried belt or pack mounted reflective shelters during this fire.

Bob Lesmeister and I met Phil Clark and Sid Burns completely by chance at Domke Lake in August of 2009, and we had an impromptu reunion. Sid now operates Gordon Stuart's old resort at Domke Lake. Previously, he worked for the Forest Service out of Chelan for many years. I also enjoyed having coffee with Doug Bowie and Tar Lesmeister in East Wenatchee last spring to verify details and events described in this book. It was fun to reminsce with Bill Moody. He provided suggestions and information that were essential to the sharing of these stories.

In conclusion, I have been reassured about the care our forests are getting while meeting and talking with many of the people who work in today's Forest Service. I am convinced that they are as much in love with their work as we were with ours many years ago. It is obvious to me that they are doing a very professional job with limited resources. The trails, camp sites and landmarks that I saw in the upper Lake Chelan area last summer are every bit as clean, beautiful and well preserved as when we cared for them fifty years ago. I encourage you to go there and see for yourself. After all, these forest lands belong to you!

Unplanned reunion of four old fire fighters at Domke Lake in 2009. Note effects across the lake of the Domke Complex Fire of 2007. (L to R) Phil Clark, Sid Burns, Bob Lesmeister and the author.

Bibliography

Books

Adams, Nigel B. *The Holden Mine: Discovery to Production,* The World Publishing Company, Wenatchee, Washington, 1981.

Bryant, Sandy K.Nelson. Mountain Air: *The Life of Gordon Stuart — Mountain Man of the North Cascades.* Webco Publications. Wenatchee, Washington. 1986.

Byrd, Robert. *Lake Chelan in the 1890s.* The World Publishing Company. Wenatchee, Washington. 1972.

Egan, Timothy. *The Big Burn.* Houghton Mifflin Harcourt. New York. 2009.

Kresek, Ray. *Fire Lookouts of the Northwest.* Ye Galleon Press. 1984.

Gregg, Kristen J. *Images of America — Lake Chelan Valley.* Arcadia Publishing. Charleston, SC. 2009.

Mikesh, Robert C. *Japan's World War 11 Balloon Bomb Attacks on North America.* Smithsonian Institute Press.1978

Maclean, John N. *Fire on the Mountain.* William Morrow and Company. New York. 1999.

Maclean, John N. *The Thirtymile Fire.* Henry Holt and Company. New York. 2007.

Maclean, Norman. *Young Men and Fire.* University of Chicago Press. Chicago, Illinois. 1992.

Matthews, Mark. *Smokejumping on the Western Fire Line.* University of Oklahoma Press. Norman. 2006.

Matthews, Mark. *A Great Day to Fight Fire — Mann Gulch,* 1949. University of Oklahoma Press. Norman. 2007.

Moody, Bill and Longley, Larry. *Spittin' in the Wind.* National Smoke-jumper Association. Missoula, Montana. 2007.

Pyne, Stephen. *Year of the Fires.* Penguin Putnam, Inc. new York. 2001

Spring, Ira and Fish, Byron. *Lookouts.* The Mountaineers. Seattle. 1981.

Taylor, Murray. *Jumping Fire.* Harcourt, Inc. New York. 2000.

Yaar, Warren. *Smokechaser.* University of Idaho Press. 1995.

Articles

Chelan Leader. "Holden Mine Looks Better." 1909

Chelan Valley Mirror. July 21, 1960. "Platt, England Injured in Helicopter Crash."

Ibid. August 4, 1960. "Leo England, A.K. Platt At Home."

Ibid. July 9, 1964. "Platt is Killed In Copter."

Ibid. July 10, 1964. "Helicopter Crash Remains A Mystery."

Wenatchee Daily World. August 1963. "Glasses Fall Out of Plane, Unbroken."

Research Paper

Undated. J. David Rogers, PhD, P.E., R.G., C.E.G., C.HG. Chair in Geological Engineering. Missouri University of Science and Technology. How Geologists Unraveled the Mystery of Japanese Vengeance Balloon Bombs in WW11. http://web.mst.edu/~rogersda/forensic_geology/ Japanese%20vengeance%20bombs%20.

Unpublished Reports

Blair, J. K. *Fire Warehouse and Aerial Tanker Base.* Wenatchee National
Forest. Region 6. 1962.

Deleon, Mark. *Chronology of the Okanogon National Forest.* Feb. 1989.

Other Sources

Personal interviews and discussions with former and current Forest
Service personnel including Mario A. Faletto, Sim Beeson and numerous others. Chelan, Washington. 1955 through 1965.

Personal interview and discussions with Major Hugo W. Schott, USAF,
Commander. Naselle Air Force Station, Washington. August 1965.

Personal interview with Hugo W. Schott via telephone. San Antonio,
Texas. June 2005.

Personal interviews, via telephone and/or email with Bill Moody, Tom
Lueschen, Barry George, Linda Martinson, Mallory Lenz, Bob Sheehan,
Bob Lesmeister, Doug Bowie, Tar Lesmeister, Roger Stafford, Jim
Theubet, Powys Gadd, Susan Peterson, Cindy Mitchell, Butch Croy,
Phil Clark and Jim Paulson. Sandpoint, Idaho. June 2007; April 2010;
Sandpoint, Idaho.

Reference Notes

Introduction

U.S. Army Air Corps first mobile radar unit and P-38s stationed at Comox RCAFB, Vancouver Island, BC. Interviews with Lt. Col. Hugo W. Schott, USAF, Retired. August, 1965 and June 2005.

Japanese Fire Balloons. Mikesh, Robert C. *Japan's WW11 Balloon Bomb Attacks on North America.1978.* J. David Rogers, PhD. *How Geologists Unravelled the Mystery of Japanese Vengeance Balloon Bombs in WW11.* Interviews with Mario A. Faletto, Chief of Police, Chelan, Washington. July, 1955 and August 1965.

U.S. Army Firefly Project and 555th Parachute Infantry Battalion. *Spittin' In The Wind.* Moody and Langley. 2007.

First jumps on active fires. *Ibid.*

Chapter One

"Tsillane". *Lake Chelan in the 1890s.* Byrd, Robert.1972.

Lake Chelan and Chelan River characteristics and statistics. *Ibid.*

Stehekin, Indian name for "the way through." *Ibid.*

Mining activity in Holden and in Horseshoe Basin. *Ibid.*

Chelan Ranger District History. Unpublished reports. Mark Deleon. Feb 1989. Mallory Lenz. March 2010.

"A most beautiful trip up this lovely lake." *The Big Burn*. Timothy Egan. 2009.

Chapter Two

Wagner Dodge and Mann Gulch backfire. *Young Men and Fire*. Norman Maclean.1992. *A Great Day to Fight Fire-Mann Gulch, 1949*. Mark Matthews. 2007.

Number Two Canyon Fire and AK Platt' crash. News article, *Chelan Valley Mirror*. July 21, 1960.

AK Platt's fatal crash on Joe Creek. News article, *Chelan Valley Mirror*. July 9, 1964.

Chapter Three

Oscar Getty and Gordon Stuart. *Mountain Air: The Life of Gordon Stuart — Mountain Man*. Bryant, Sandy K. Nelson.1986.

Chapter Five

Ibid.

Chapter Six

Lucerne. *Images of America-Lake Chelan Valley*. Kristen J. Gregg.2009

Chapter Seven

Lutheran Church and Holden Village. *Ibid*.

Lutheran Church and Holden Village. *The Holden Mine: Discovery to Production*. Nigel Adams. 1981.

Chapter Eight

Crown Point, Lyman Lake and Lyman Cabin. *Images of America — Lake Chelan Valley*. Kristen J. Gregg. 2009.

Chapters Sixteen through Twenty

Aerial Tanker Base. Unpublished Report. J. K. Blair. 1962.

Made in the USA
Charleston, SC
12 June 2010